Politics and Morality

Published

Akbar Ahmed, Islam under Siege
Zygmunt Bauman, Community
Zygmunt Bauman, Europe
Zygmunt Bauman, Globalization
Zygmunt Bauman, Identity
Richard Bernstein, The Abuse of Evil
Norberto Bobbio, Left and Right
Alex Callinicos, Equality
Diane Coyle, Governing the World Economy
Colin Crouch, Post-Democracy
David Crystal, The Language Revolution
Andrew Gamble, Politics and Fate
Conor Gearty, Liberty and Security
Paul Hirst, War and Power in the 21st Century
Bill Jordan and Franck Düvell, Migration
David Lyon, Surveillance after September 11
James Mayall, World Politics
Tariq Modood, Multiculturalism
Ray Pahl, On Friendship
Robert Reiner, Law and Order
Christian Reus-Smit, American Power and World Order
Shaun Riordan, The New Diplomacy

Politics and Morality

Susan Mendus

polity

first years of the twenty-first century have been distinguished by an explosion of immorality and duplicity
amongst politicians, and similar concerns about the politics of the United States can be found in a large number
of publications, of which Eric Alterman's *When Presidents
Lie: A History of Political Deception and Its Consequences*
(2005) and Larry Flynt's *Sex, Lies and Politics: The Naked
Truth about Bush, Democracy and the War on Terror* (2005)
are just two. It is, I think, questionable whether the rise
of political lying has been quite as meteoric as these writers
claim. As we have seen, the fact that politicians can be
self-serving was well known, and guarded against, even
in Aristotle's day. Beyond that, however, the claim that
modern-day politicians do, as a matter of fact, lie in order
to further their own interests can serve to disguise a deeper
and more important question – the question which is
central to this book – namely, whether the very structure
of politics itself is such as to demand lying.[1]

central
questions

There are in fact two questions here: first, whether
politicians are especially likely to be called upon to act
immorally (to lie, to deceive, to mislead); second, whether
we can reasonably expect that those who are willing to lie
in order to further the interests of the state will be able to
refrain from lying when it is in their own interest to do so.
Much modern commentary on the relationship between
morality and politics takes as central the proposition that
politics *as a profession* regularly and reliably calls for morally
disreputable behaviour. In doing so, it does not focus on
self-serving lying, or on what has come to be known as
'sleaze'. Rather, it focuses on cases in which there are, or
seem to be, important *political* reasons for lying and where,
therefore, a politician's refusal or inability to lie might
be tantamount to an inability to perform his[2] duties as a
politician. An example may serve to highlight the precise
nature of the problem.

In 1959, Fidel Castro overthrew General Batista to become President of Cuba. Initially, Castro had hoped to obtain support for his regime from the United States, which had been opposed to Batista's rule. However, as businesses and industries in Cuba were nationalized, and thus taken away from their private owners (who were often American), the USA imposed trade embargoes on Cuba and finally cut off diplomatic relations. Faced with the withdrawal of US support, Castro looked elsewhere and found a willing ally in the Soviet Union under Khrushchev. The USSR was willing to buy the Cuban sugar no longer wanted by the United States and Cuba's economic position improved dramatically through the relationship with the USSR. In 1962, Castro sanctioned the installation of forty Soviet missiles on Cuba, and the USA retaliated by making ready nuclear weapons for launch on the island. This was what came to be known as the 'Cuban Missile Crisis', which ended in late October when Khrushchev agreed to withdraw Soviet weapons from Cuba on condition that the USA undertook not to invade the island. It subsequently came to light that in discussions with Khrushchev, President Kennedy not only promised that the USA would not invade Cuba, but also promised that the USA would remove its missiles from Turkey. Strictly speaking, this was not a deal because well before the crisis Kennedy had ordered the removal of missiles from Turkey anyway. However, Khrushchev needed to present it as part of a deal in order to win over his hard-line colleagues in the USSR, and Kennedy needed to say nothing about it in order to deflect the possibility that it would be seen as yielding to pressure from the USSR.[3] On the face of it, this was a case in which political security could be attained only by deception on the part of both Khrushchev and Kennedy. And both did deceive. Of course, their deception served to keep them in power but, beyond that, deception was necessary in order to secure peace between the two great political powers of the Cold War period and to avert war.

As told, this story is one in which politics itself demanded deceit and duplicity: it is a case in which politicians were required to lie in order to preserve the political order which it was their duty, as politicians, to preserve. So, Khrushchev and Kennedy may have had a moral duty, as human beings, to refrain from lying, but in this case they also had a duty, as politicians, to deceive or mislead. It is this kind of conflict between the demands of morality (ordinarily understood) and the demands of politics that is the central focus of this book. More precisely, my central question is whether the kind of conflict manifest in the Cuban Missile Crisis is predictable in and characteristic of politics. Bernard Williams offers an affirmative answer when he says: '[I]t is a predictable and probable hazard of public life that there will be situations in which something morally disagreeable is clearly required. To refuse on moral grounds ever to do anything of that sort is more than likely to mean that one cannot seriously pursue even the moral ends of politics' (Williams, 1981, p. 60).

Why might this be so? Why might politics *itself* call for deceit? One answer, an answer suggested by the Cuban example, is that what matters in politics is getting the right result, where getting the right result may involve doing something which is usually considered wrong. This thought is often expressed via the slogan 'the end justifies the means'. If politics is indeed an area in which the end justifies the means, then those who elect to become politicians are thereby indicating their willingness to do whatever is necessary to secure the ends of politics and thus to disregard, or at least marginalize, questions about the morality of the means they use in order to attain those results.

There is, however, a complication to this story: even if we accept that politics is a matter of getting results, and even if we also accept that getting results may, from time to time, mean adopting morally dubious means, we may also be reluctant to elect those who announce in advance their disregard for the morality of means. Here is an example, taken from Michael Walzer:

> Consider a politician who has seized upon a national crisis – a prolonged colonial war – to reach for power. He and his friends win office pledged to decolonization and peace: they are honestly committed to both, though not without some sense of the advantages of the commitment. In any case, they have no responsibility for the war; they have steadfastly opposed it. Immediately, the politician goes off to the colonial capital to open negotiations with the rebels. But the capital is in the grip of a terrorist campaign, and the first decision the new leader faces is this: he is asked to authorize the torture of a captured rebel leader who knows or probably knows the location of a number of bombs hidden in apartment buildings around the city, set to go off within the next twenty-four hours. He orders the man tortured, convinced that he must do so for the sake of the people who might otherwise die in the explosions – even though he believes that torture is wrong, indeed abominable, and not just sometimes, but always. He had expressed this belief often and angrily during his own campaign; the rest of us took it as a sign of his goodness. How should we regard him now? How should he regard himself? (Walzer, 1974, pp. 68–9)

Walzer's example draws attention to the fact that, even if the profession of politics calls for a willingness to do whatever is necessary in order to attain the right results, politicians themselves are elected because they have (or are thought to have) moral principles. The politician in his example is a man who has 'dirty hands', both in the sense that he has done what he believes to be wrong, and in the

the case of Heinrich Himmler, who, during World War II, became leader of the SS and, in that capacity, commanded the entire concentration-camp system and was responsible for the execution of the 'final solution of the Jewish problem'. In a speech made to some SS generals, Himmler said:

> What happens to a Russian, a Czech, does not interest me in the slightest. What the nations can offer in the way of good blood of our type, we will take, if necessary by kidnapping their children and raising them here with us. Whether nations live in prosperity or starve to death like cattle interests me only in so far as we need them as slaves to our *Kultur*; otherwise it is of no interest to me. Whether 10,000 Russian females fall down from exhaustion while digging an antitank ditch interests me only in so far as the antitank ditch for Germany is finished. (as quoted in Shirer, 1991, pp. 937–8)

On this, and other, evidence, there is no denying that Himmler was a man who knew what he stood for and had settled reasons for taking the stand he did. He was not a crowd-follower, nor was he whimsical or capricious. In short, he satisfied the conditions for integrity as they are specified in the integrated-self picture. However, it is hard to see why integrity, so understood, is a good thing, and it is even harder to see why we should be troubled by the possibility that politics undermines integrity. We might well think that, although Himmler certainly was a man of integrity, the world would have been a better place had he lacked integrity. So, the conviction that integrity is a virtue and that we should be concerned about the way in which it is undermined by politics cannot adequately be explained by the integrated-self account of integrity, which focuses

on the agent's steadfastness and fidelity to his own principles but is indifferent as to whether those principles are
morally good ones.

Identity

Similar problems surface, though in a rather different
guise, with the second picture of integrity – the identity
picture. On this account, integrity is a matter of having a
character and being true to it. Like the integrated-self
picture, this picture emphasizes the fact that a person of
integrity will have principles which are his own and which
he resolutely adheres to. However, the identity picture
goes beyond the integrated-self picture in its insistence
that loss of integrity is, in some part, loss of oneself.
On this account, it is not simply one's principles that
are lost when integrity is sacrificed; it is one's *self*, one's
understanding of who one is. To see what is at stake
here, consider the following example taken from Bernard
Williams' 'A Critique of Utilitarianism':

> George, who has just taken his PhD in Chemistry, finds it
> extremely difficult to get a job. He is not very robust in
> health, which cuts down the number of jobs he might be
> able to do satisfactorily. His wife has to go out to work to
> keep them, which itself causes a great deal of strain, since
> they have small children and there are severe problems
> about looking after them....An older chemist, who knows
> about this situation, says that he can get George a decently
> paid job in a certain laboratory, which pursues research
> into chemical and biological warfare. George says that he
> cannot accept this, since he is opposed to chemical and
> biological warfare. The older man replies that he is not too
> keen on it himself, come to that, but after all George's
> refusal is not going to make the job or the laboratory go
> away; what is more, he happens to know that if George

refuses the job, it will certainly go to a contemporary of George's who is not inhibited by any such scruples and who is likely if appointed to push along the research with greater zeal than George would. Indeed, it is not merely concern for George but...some alarm about this other man's excess of zeal, which has led the older man to offer to use his influence to get George the job....George's wife, to whom he is deeply attached, has views (the details of which need not concern us) from which it follows that at least there is nothing particularly wrong with research into CBW. What should he do? (Williams, 1973, pp. 97–8)

Williams' example is offered as part of his critique of utilitarianism and it is intended to show that utilitarianism makes integrity as a value unintelligible. I will discuss this aspect of the example in Chapter 3. For now, however, I invoke it simply in order to explain what the identity picture of integrity is and how it differs from the integrated-self picture. Having offered the example, Williams goes on to comment:

The point is that he [George] is identified with his actions as flowing from projects and attitudes which in some cases he takes seriously at the deepest level, as what his life is about...it is absurd to demand of such a man, when the sums come in from the utility network which the projects of others have in part determined, that he should just step aside from his own project and decision and acknowledge the decision which utilitarian calculation requires. It is to alienate him in a real sense from his actions and the source of his actions in his own commitments. It is to make him into a channel between the input of everyone's projects, including his own, and an output of optimific decision; but this is to neglect the extent to which *his* actions and *his* decisions have to be seen as the actions and decisions which flow from the projects and attitudes with which he is most closely identified. It is thus, in the most literal sense, an attack on his integrity. (Williams, 1973, pp. 116–17)

Whereas the integrated-self picture of integrity emphasizes the fact that a person of integrity has his own settled and considered principles, and that he acts on those principles for his own reasons, the identity picture goes further and construes integrity as a matter of acting on principles which are not merely one's own, but which *define who one is.* Hence Williams' insistence that, in the example given, it will not be merely disagreeable for George to abandon his principles; it will be an attack on his own sense of himself.

As with the integrated-self picture, so here we should note that there is no requirement that the principles or commitments that go to make up a person's integrity shall be morally admirable. We may or may not share George's disapproval of chemical and biological warfare, but the crucial point is not whether we think that George's projects are morally worthy projects; the crucial point is that they are *George's* projects and, for better or worse, if he were to abandon them he would (in the example given) lose his sense of who he is. He would lose his integrity, understood in the identity-conferring sense. So, to return to the example of Himmler given earlier, we might think that it would be a thoroughly good thing were Himmler to abandon his deep commitment to the 'final solution' and thus to sacrifice his integrity either in the integrated-self or in the identity sense. In neither case do integrity and moral goodness go hand-in-hand. But the fact that they do not go hand in hand makes it difficult to understand why the possibility that politics undermines integrity must be problematic.

Moreover, the identity picture of integrity gives rise to a further problem above and beyond the problems

identified with the integrated-self picture of integrity. This
is that, by placing so much emphasis on the agent's sense
of himself and on the significance of his own projects, the
identity picture can appear to be simply a defence of nar-
cissism. Even if we allow that George's hatred of CBW is
wholly admirable, we might nonetheless wonder whether
his identity is destroyed through involvement with it and
we may also think that, even if it is, that is not necessarily
the worst thing in the world. We might, for instance, note
that, in the example given, his sense of self can be retained
only by sacrificing the well-being of his wife and children,
and we might feel that, so understood, integrity is not
necessarily an admirable quality to have.

Clean hands

The problems associated with the integrated-self picture
and the identity picture of integrity prompt the move to a
third picture – the clean hands picture of integrity. On this
picture, and to quote Calhoun, 'a person has integrity
when there are some things she will not do regardless of
the consequences of refusal. In bottom-line situations, she
places the importance of principle and the purity of her
own agency above consequentialist concerns' (Calhoun,
1995, p. 246). Thus, to return again to Walzer's initial
example, for the politician to be a person of integrity is for
him to refuse to co-operate with the evil that is torture,
and to refuse to do so even when the consequences of
refusing are very bad indeed. It is because, in advance of
the election, the politician has given an assurance that he
will have no truck with torture that he now feels his con-
donation of it constitutes a sacrifice of integrity. It is a case
in which he has said that there are some things which are
absolutely wrong and which he will never do, but politics
forces him to do (or at least to consider doing) those

things. It forces him to associate with what he believes to be evil. Calhoun argues that the clean hands account of integrity is superior to the other two just because and insofar as it enables us to see how a person's integrity is not merely tied up with his principles, his commitments, or his sense of himself; it is also tied up with what he believes to be morally wrong. She says, 'It captures...the kind of thinking we expect behind principled refusals – not, "I couldn't go on as the same person if I did this" but "I would be doing a wrong"' (Calhoun, 1995, p. 246). Of course, different people have different moral beliefs and, as has been noted, Himmler's moral beliefs are not ones which many share. Nonetheless, there is an important difference between accounts of integrity which trace it to the agent's sense of himself, and accounts of integrity which trace it to moral convictions – convictions about the way the world should be rather than convictions about how the agent should be.

The differences between these three pictures of integrity can be most clearly understood if we consider what, under each account, a loss of integrity amounts to. On the integrated-self view, loss of integrity consists (in part) in yielding to the opinions of others and thus allowing myself to become less of a coherent whole. Crudely put, when I lose integrity on this account I cease to act on my own values and substitute the values of others. On the identity picture, loss of integrity is tantamount to loss of oneself: it arises in circumstances in which I abandon my ground projects and thereby cease to exist as the same person. Finally, the clean hands picture construes loss of integrity as a matter of allowing myself to be implicated in what I consider to be evil. It is only this last conception that introduces the notion of moral wrongness, and it is for this reason that Calhoun finds it more satisfactory than the other two accounts. However, even here it must be stressed that the

The force of that charge was not that he had failed to sustain (or had misrepresented) the boundaries of his self. The force of the charge was that he had treated as a matter of little significance the representation and defence of views that in one's own best judgement are the better ones. He did so either by misrepresenting his own view of the ban in the first place or by too readily conceding to a view he considered wrong. This, in the eyes of his critics, constituted less a self-betrayal than a betrayal of those counting on him to stand up for what they took to be the better view. Moreover, not standing up for one's best judgement about what would be just or what lives are acceptable forms of the good suggests that it does not really matter what we as a community of reasoners endorse. The person of integrity, one might plausibly think, is precisely the person who thinks this does matter. Integrity here seems tightly connected to viewing oneself as a member of an evaluating community and caring about what that community endorses. That is, it seems to be a social virtue. (p. 254)

My own view is that those who criticized Clinton for lacking integrity precisely *did* think that he had betrayed himself. Of course, they were also very concerned about the practical consequences of that for them, and for the policy they believed to be the right one. What they wanted, and what they believed to be morally right, was that gays and lesbians be admitted openly to the military, but that possibility was ruled out when Clinton capitulated and (notoriously) implemented the policy commonly known as 'Don't ask, don't tell'. Undeniably, then, the members of the gay and lesbian communities were let down by President Clinton. Indeed, they were betrayed by him, and that is no small matter. When a person of huge power and influence shows, by his actions, that he cannot be relied upon to do the things he has promised to do, and on the basis of which he has secured considerable electoral support, we can be forgiven for wondering whether he actually has any principles at all, and it is this, I suggest, that constitutes the heart of the integrity problem, for what mattered to Clinton's critics was not simply, as Calhoun alleges, that he betrayed *them* and that, in so doing, he implied that he had no regard for the community of reasoners. What mattered was that he betrayed *himself* and thus brought into question *his own* status as a person of principle.

To put the point slightly differently, if someone lacks integrity (or loses integrity), then it is of course a consequence of that fact that he cannot be relied upon by the rest of us, but the essence of integrity lies not in the fact that others can depend upon me, but rather in the fact that they can depend upon me because I know who I am and what my ethical commitments are. If integrity were, as Calhoun insists, a matter of standing for something before others, then integrity would be preserved just insofar as I can justify my behaviour to others, but, from the agent's own point of view, the ability to defend his actions to others is distinct from the ability to defend his actions to himself. It is, I think, this latter that is central to integrity, but in order to defend that claim fully I need now to say a bit more about the relationship between integrity and morality.

Integrity and morality

The discussion so far has focused on three pictures of integrity identified by Calhoun. These are: the integrated-self picture, the identity picture, and the clean hands picture. In all three cases integrity is distinct from moral goodness, and on all three accounts people who exhibit integrity may nonetheless be morally bad. This, however, is puzzling because integrity is normally thought to be a virtue and, if it is a virtue, it is hard to see how and why we might be glad if some people (Himmler, for example) fail to display it.

But if we have reason to be glad that people do not always display integrity, we may also have reason to be glad that people do not always obey the dictates of morality. In the quotation which stands at the head of this chapter, Bernard Williams defines integrity as a matter of standing by what one believes to be ethically necessary. The word 'ethically' is important because it points to a distinction between different kinds of value: it suggests that there may not be simply one distinctively moral value, but different kinds of broadly ethical values, some of which reflect the agent's own beliefs and commitments, and which are associated with his or her integrity, while others reflect the values of society, or of what Calhoun calls 'the community of reasoners', and are associated with social or conventional morality. Moreover, just as we may sometimes be glad if people (like Himmler) do not retain their integrity, so we may sometimes be glad if people do not adhere to the dictates of social or conventional morality.

To see how this might happen, recall the case of George, who is offered a job in a laboratory which specializes in research into chemical and biological warfare. George has strong objections to chemical and biological warfare and, for that reason, is very reluctant to accept the job. However, he is also deeply committed to his wife and children, and is aware that if he does not take the job the consequences for them will be extremely damaging. In addition, he has been told that if he does not take the job, someone else will, and the consequences of that will be that the research is likely to be conducted more efficiently and effectively than it would be if George were in charge. Avoiding involvement in chemical and biological warfare is, we are told, 'ethically necessary' for George; it is a matter of 'sticking by' his commitments and refusing to engage in what he believes to be evil. However, on at least some accounts, if George were to refuse to engage in research into chemical and biological warfare, he would behave morally badly. He would show disregard for the interests of his family and of the wider community, all of whom will be worse off if he refuses the job than if he takes it. So, what we seem to have here is a case in which integrity, understood as sticking by what one believes to be ethically necessary and refusing to engage in evil, requires that George refuse the job, whereas morality, understood as taking account of the consequences of our actions for others and of our responsibilities to them, requires that George accept the job.

It may seem that in this case the tension between integrity and morality is created by adopting a conception of morality that places great weight on consequences, but in fact the problem is wider than that and is generated not merely by consequentialist understandings of morality, but by impartialist understandings of morality – that is to say, by conceptions of morality that insist on the importance of treating all equally or of showing equal respect for everyone. This tension is not an accident. Impartialist morality, whether consequentialist or not, is a very important way of restricting a person's ability to act on his or her personal commitments, or on what he or she believes to be ethically necessary, so the tension between integrity (understood as a matter of sticking by what one believes to be ethically necessary) and morality (understood as acting impartially towards all who are affected by one's actions) is both predictable and unavoidable in ways I will now try to spell out.

There are two features of morality that are widely noted in the literature, and both serve to highlight the reasons why integrity and morality may be in tension with one another. The first (already alluded to) is that morality is impartial; the second is that it has 'trumping power' over other considerations. In the opening pages of *A Theory of Justice*, John Rawls writes:

> Justice is the first virtue of social institutions as truth is of systems of thought...each person possesses an inviolability founded on justice that even the welfare of society as a whole cannot override. For this reason, justice denies that the loss of freedom for some is made right by a greater good shared by others. It does not allow that the sacrifices imposed on a few are outweighed by the larger sum of advantages enjoyed by many...being first virtues of human activities, truth and justice are uncompromising. (Rawls, 1971, p. 3)

Rawls' claim that justice is uncompromising constitutes a statement of his premises. He offers no argument for this claim; it is simply the background against which the arguments of *A Theory of Justice* are put forward. And the claim contains two thoughts. The first is that justice in particular and morality in general demand impartiality: everyone has the same rights and liberties independent of their social class, religion, gender, or race. The second is that these requirements are more important than any other requirements. They are 'trumping' requirements (they are 'uncompromising'). Simply put, the claim is that the demands of impartial morality matter more than the demands made by our personal, or partial, commitments. It is more important to be fair to all people, to treat all equally, than it is to look after the interests of my friends and family. And yet, we often have very strong desires to favour our friends and family over others, and often there is nothing wrong with this. If I throw a party, I am free to invite whomever I want and there is no requirement to treat everyone equally. People may legitimately be invited simply because they are my friends, I like them, and I want to spend time with them. Conversely, they may be excluded because they are not my friends, I find them dull and boring, and I do not wish to spend time with them. However, the requirement that morality be impartial and that it have trumping power is an attempt to set limits to these exercises of favouritism or partiality. So, to give an example, when I arrange individual tutorials for my students, I am not entitled to exclude some students on the grounds that I don't like them, nor am I entitled to offer more help to the students I like than to the students I dislike, or am indifferent to. Giving parties is one thing; giving tutorials is another, and part of the point of social or conventional morality is to set limits to my ability to favour my friends or family over others.

The examples are trivial in themselves, but they raise important questions about the relationship between integrity and morality. In particular, they draw attention to the fact that morality, with its requirement of impartiality, is an attempt to set limits to my ability to act on my own projects or commitments, or on what I believe to be ethically necessary. So, even though it is the case that I love my friends and the members of my family more than others, and even though it is true that my commitment to them is something that gives meaning to my life and partly defines who I am, it is also the case that there are limits to the extent to which I may give priority to their needs and interests, and morality is a way of setting those limits.

The implications of this for integrity are very great: I have argued that integrity is a matter of acting on those commitments which are very important to me and which serve, in part, to define who I am, but I have also noted that morality is a way of restricting my ability to act on commitments which matter very much to me and which define who I am. It follows from these two thoughts that morality (impartial morality) is at odds with integrity and, at least in principle, has a tendency to undermine it. How, then, should we respond to cases in which integrity and morality conflict with one another? The case of Himmler suggested that, at least sometimes, we should be glad if people abandon integrity and adhere to the dictates of morality. Are there also cases in which we have reason to be glad if people abandon morality in order to retain integrity? I think that there are, and that the reasons are two-fold. Firstly, it may be that without the values and commitments which constitute our integrity, we would not be able to acknowledge the importance of morality. In other words, if we ask why people are motivated to act in accordance with the dictates of morality, we may find that our answer makes essential reference to the values and commitments which constitute their integrity. So integrity may be needed for the recognition and cultivation of morality (Mendus, 2008).

Secondly, it is often the case that the values which constitute someone's integrity are themselves ethically important. So, for example, my friends and family are extremely important to me; I care about them very much and my love for them is partly definitive of who I am. But love for friends and family is not only a natural tendency, nor is it something which always conflicts with the values of morality; it is also morally worthy and morally significant in itself. To see this, note that I have special duties (moral duties) towards my friends and family such that if, for instance, my children's school were to catch fire, I would be *morally* entitled (and perhaps even morally required) to help them before helping others. In other words, then, some partial values, such as loyalty to friends and family, can be both constitutive of integrity and a demand of impartial morality, and any sensible form of impartial morality will allow for the fact that those values which go to make up people's integrity may themselves be values which are morally worthy. To the extent that this is so, a demand to sacrifice integrity to morality should be treated with caution, since it may be that the retention of the values which constitute integrity is a condition of being able to recognize and respond to the demands of morality in the first place. And it may also be that any attack on integrity is an attack on the motivational foundation of impartial morality.

To highlight what is at stake here, consider Lynne McFall's discussion of a case in which, as captain of a sinking ship, I am called upon to save people who are drowning, and I have time to save either two complete strangers or my husband, but not both. McFall argues that such a case displays a tension within morality and, in particular, a tension between what she calls personal morality, on the one hand, and social morality, on the other. She writes:

> Whatever choice I make I would not be morally blame-worthy. If I save the two strangers, I am right from the social-moral point of view; if I save my husband, I am right from the personal-moral point of view. And whatever choice I make I am wrong from some point of view. Since both are moral requirements of comparable importance, I am free to choose, based on commitments particular to myself, what I could or could not 'live with' (or without). (McFall, 1987, p. 19)

Pace McFall, it seems to me that, if I am the captain of the ship, and I save my husband in preference to two

other people, then I am indeed blameworthy, because I
have failed to execute one of the most serious obligations
associated with being captain of a ship. I have abandoned
my passengers. Of course, we may all understand why
someone would act in that way, and we may all hope never
to be in such a position ourselves. That said, though, questions of integrity are different from questions of blame,
and it may be that there are cases where one's integrity
can be preserved only by doing things which properly
incur blame. In the example just given, it may be that the
dilemma I face when the ship begins to sink is one that
prompts me to ask what is most important to me – my
family or my role as captain of the ship. Suppose that I
come to realize that the values of the family are more
important to me than the duties associated with my role
as ship's captain. If that were the case, then to abandon
my husband would constitute a serious loss of integrity
and I might decide that I would prefer to be held morally
blameworthy by others than to lose integrity in that way.

However, it might be that when the ship begins to sink,
I decide to save the two strangers. It now seems that my
role as ship's captain is what really matters to me and,
although I am desolate at the prospect of losing my
husband, I nonetheless abandon him in order to fulfil the
duties of my office. In saving the strangers, I act in accordance with what impartial morality dictates, but we may
wonder what kind of person could bring herself to do this,
and we may conclude that, if this is what morality demands,
it is not always or necessarily a good thing that people
behave morally well. Just as in the case of Himmler we
wondered whether the world would be a better place if
people did not always have integrity, so here we may
wonder whether the world would be a better place if
people did not always act in accordance with the dictates
of impartial morality.

Conclusion

The aim of this chapter has been to explain what integrity is. I began by saying that in order to understand whether integrity is more difficult for politicians, we first need to decide what integrity is for any of us – whether politicians or not.

My discussion of integrity began with the three pictures of integrity identified by Calhoun. These are the integrated-self picture, the identity picture, and the clean hands picture. Calhoun rejects all these in favour of an understanding of integrity as a matter of standing for something before co-deliberators, and her aim in doing this is to show how integrity is a social and not merely a personal virtue. However, I am doubtful about this strategy, primarily because I don't myself think that integrity is essentially a social virtue. My own belief is that morality stands in contrast to integrity insofar as it consists in an attempt to restrain our inclinations to act on our own concerns, commitments, and values. In short, morality asks us to act on impartial reasons, whereas integrity consists in acting on *our own* reasons, and our own reasons are often partial rather than impartial. When they are partial, a conflict arises between morality and integrity.

The discussion so far should enable us to see that neither integrity nor morality is an unalloyed good. In some cases, such as the case of Himmler, we may think that the world would be a better place if people lacked integrity; and in other cases, such as the case of the ship's captain who saves the strangers rather than her husband, we may think that the world would be a better place if people sometimes failed to be moral. Morality and integrity reflect different, and conflicting, values. Or so it seems.

Integrity, then, is a matter of standing by one's most fundamental ethical commitments, where those commitments may or may not be the same as the commitments of impartial morality. A person who loses or sacrifices integrity will feel both that he has abandoned the values he stands for and that he has associated with evil. The question now is whether and why integrity, so understood, is more difficult for politicians than for the rest of us. It is this question that will be the focus of the next chapter.

2

Political Integrity

It is a predictable and probable hazard of public life that there will be these situations in which something morally disagreeable is clearly required. To refuse on moral grounds ever to do anything of that sort is more than likely to mean that one cannot pursue even the moral ends of politics.

Williams, 1981, p. 60

The previous chapter ended with a working definition of integrity as a matter of standing by one's most fundamental ethical commitments, where those commitments may or may not be compatible with the dictates of morality, impartially understood. As we have seen, the possibility of tension between integrity and impartial morality arises because part of the function of morality is to constrain our ability to act on our own commitments, whereas integrity is defined precisely as a matter of acting on those commitments. Conflict between integrity and morality is therefore a permanent possibility.

That said, however, we should also note that many of our most fundamental commitments – commitments to friends and family, for instance – are, in themselves, both admirable and morally legitimate. It is often the case that a person's commitments to her friends and family are amongst the most fundamental in her life, and it is also the case that acting on those commitments by giving priority to one's friends or family is perfectly acceptable, indeed desirable, from a moral point of view. Recall the case of the private person who finds herself on a sinking ship and able to save either her husband or two complete strangers, but not both. Normally, we would think that such a person is perfectly entitled to favour her husband over the strangers and indeed we may even think that someone who did not do so was both morally and emotionally defective. There is nothing morally wrong about having fundamental ethical commitments to members of one's family and there is nothing inherently wrong about giving preference to members of one's family over complete strangers either. It is simply that preferring one's family and friends is not always consonant with the dictates of impartial morality, and when it is not, our integrity may be threatened because we now stand under two imperatives: on the one hand, the imperative that consists in sticking by our fundamental commitments or by what we believe to be ethically necessary, and, on the other hand, the imperative that is issued by impartial morality itself. This, then, is the general form of the tension between integrity and impartial morality. It is a tension that arises when one's own, partial, projects and commitments come into conflict with the demands of morality, impartially understood.

Why might integrity, understood as a matter of standing by one's most fundamental ethical commitments, be more difficult for politicians than for other people? This is the central question of this chapter, and in order to answer it I will return to Walzer's example of the politician who has been elected to office in part by giving assurances that he will never sanction torture, but who finds, once elected, that torture is the only thing that will save the lives of many innocent people. The question now is: 'Should he sanction torture and save the lives of the innocent, thereby reneging on his promise to the electorate and also compromising his own integrity, or should he stick by his own principles and refuse to sanction the torture?' Walzer implies that the politician must sanction the torture, and, indeed, that it is only by doing so that he can claim to be a good (moral) politician. He writes:

> His willingness to acknowledge and bear (and perhaps repent and do penance for) his guilt is evidence, and it is the only evidence he can offer us, both that he is not too good for politics and that he is good enough. Here is the moral politician: it is by his dirty hands that we know him. If he were a moral man and nothing else, his hands would not be dirty; if he were a politician and nothing else, he would pretend that they were clean. (Walzer, 1974, p. 70)

It is implicit in the analysis offered by Walzer that politicians will indeed be required to sacrifice the beliefs and values they hold most deeply and, in that sense, will find that integrity is difficult to retain. This is clear in the example given, which stresses the fact that, once in power, the politician will find that he can no longer sustain his commitment to the absolute wrongness of torture. He believes torture to be absolutely wrong, he has given public assurances that he will have no truck with it, and he has come to power in part because he has given those assurances to the electorate. Once elected, however, he must at least consider authorizing torture in order to secure the political outcomes he has promised and on the basis of which he has been elected. Crucially, he must consider torture in order to secure politically important and morally desirable outcomes. Here, then, is a case in which politics undermines, or at least threatens to undermine, integrity.

Is it, however, simply a piece of bad luck that Walzer's politician finds himself in this position, or is it (somehow) structurally inherent in politics that it will threaten integrity? As noted in the Introduction, many writers think that the tension is structural, or at least non-contingent. Walzer implies as much, and the claim is explicit in the quotation from Bernard Williams given at the head of this chapter. The aim of this chapter, therefore, is to see why it might be the case that integrity is more difficult for politicians. I will proceed in the following stages. First, I will offer some general reasons for thinking that the duties associated with office are liable to threaten integrity. The considerations discussed here apply to the duties of office very generally, and are not specific to the duties associated with political office. However, in addition to these general reasons for thinking that official positions are liable to constitute a threat to integrity, there are also reasons for thinking that political office is especially likely to threaten integrity. So, having identified general reasons for thinking that office threatens integrity, I will go on to say why political office is especially problematic in this way. To anticipate, in the first case my claim will be that official roles threaten integrity because and insofar as they call for increased impartiality; and in the second case my claim will be that political office is especially likely to threaten integrity because it calls not only for heightened impartiality but also for increased attention to consequences. The requirements to act impartially and to pay great attention to consequences, when taken together, make integrity peculiarly difficult for politicians.

This is not all, however, for if it is indeed predictable that politics will undermine integrity – if it is, as Williams says, a 'predictable and probable hazard of public life' that it will demand morally disagreeable acts – then we might wonder about the character of those people who willingly embark on a political career, and (yet more) about the character of those who remain in politics and succeed in it over a long period. We might wonder whether, as Thomas Nagel (1978) puts it, politics selects for ruthlessness, or whether, as Machiavelli puts it, the prince 'must be prepared not to be virtuous' (Machiavelli, 1961, p. 48). This chapter therefore ends with some thoughts about the character of politicians and with the suggestion that although the cynicism (or 'realism') associated with Machiavelli may be tempting, it is not the only conclusion to draw. While we may see the politician as 'a man who has learned how not to be good', we may also see him as a man who has cultivated an alternative form of goodness. And we may have reason to be glad that he has cultivated that alternative form of goodness.

First, however, we should consider the reasons there are for thinking that integrity is more difficult for politicians than for the rest of us. As foreshadowed, I will take this topic in two parts: I will begin with a discussion of the ways in which the duties of office (any office) may threaten integrity; and I will then go on to consider the ways in which the office of politician might be especially problematic.

The duties of office

In an article entitled 'Ruthlessness in Public Life' Thomas Nagel says:

> If someone with an income of $2,000 a year trains a gun on someone with an income of $100,000 a year and makes him hand over his wallet, that is robbery. If the federal government withholds a portion of the second person's salary and gives some of it to the first person in the form

often – and legitimately – give preference to my friends or
family. Indeed, I may be morally obliged to do so. The
two points are connected. It is in part *because* office brings
power that it also brings a responsibility to act impartially
and to treat all equally. And, we might suppose, the greater
the power, the greater the responsibility to acknowledge,
and give priority to, the claims of impartiality even when
(perhaps especially when) they conflict with one's own,
partial, concerns and commitments.

Duties of office are, then, liable to threaten integrity,
and they are liable to do so because official positions
bring moral duties with them, and those moral duties
include duties of impartiality which may conflict with the
more partial commitments which invest our lives with
meaning, and which are also, and in themselves, sources
of obligation.

The duties of politics

However, if official positions are, in general, a threat to
integrity, why might political positions be especially threat-
ening in this respect? Again, Nagel suggests an answer to
this question when he writes:

> Two types of concern determine the content of morality:
> concern with what will happen and concern with what one
> is doing. Insofar as principles of conduct are determined
> by the first consideration, they will be consequentialist,
> requiring that we promote the best overall results. Insofar
> as they are determined by the second, the influence of
> consequences will be limited by certain restrictions on the
> means to be used and by a loosening of the requirement
> that one always pursues the best results. (Nagel, 1978,
> pp. 82–3)

And he goes on to suggest that political life is, in part, characterized by its emphasis on impartiality coupled with its increased attention to consequences. He notes that 'consequentialist considerations, together with impartiality, play a special role in the moral assessment of and justification of institutions', and suggests that, insofar as this is so, the people who act as agents of those institutions have an increased responsibility to attend to consequences: 'within the appropriate limits, public decisions will be justifiably more consequentialist than private ones', he says. Politics is about getting results, and it follows from this that the institutions of political life must be organized so as to secure results, and that the people who serve in those institutions (politicians, policy makers, civil servants) must pay great attention to questions of outcome and efficiency. Crudely, they must 'within appropriate limits' be more interested in the ends than in the means.

The point is a familiar one, but both its status and its implications for the moral character of politicians are vexed. The reasons for this are two-fold: first, because it is only 'within the appropriate limits' that greater attention to consequences is legitimate – and there may be no obvious way of telling what those appropriate limits are; second, because the long-term effects of acting with a heightened concern for consequences may make the agent inclined to do what is disagreeable even when it is not necessary. The first is a point about the relationship between political office and consideration of consequences; the second is a point about the relationship between political office and moral character.

To illustrate the first point, consider Thomas Jefferson's purchase of Louisiana in 1803.[1] In 1783, France had ceded Louisiana to Spain, but when, in 1800, Napoleon demanded its return, Spain complied and signed the

Treaty of Ildefonoso. The return of Louisiana to France was a source of immense anxiety to Jefferson, who believed that it would force the United States to ally itself with Great Britain and thus to lose economic, political, and social independence. Jefferson wrote:

> The cession of Louisiana and the Floridas by Spain to France works most sorely on the United States. The day that France takes possession of New Orleans fixes the sentence which is to restrain her forever within her low-water mark. It seals the union of two nations, who, in conjunction, can maintain exclusive possession of the ocean. From that moment, we must marry ourselves with the British fleet and nation. (as quoted in Newbold, 2005, p. 670)

Jefferson therefore took action. He sent Monroe and Livingston to negotiate on behalf of the United States for the purchase of New Orleans and Florida only, and he was therefore astonished to hear that they had not only received, but had accepted, an offer from Napoleon for the purchase of the whole of Louisiana at an exceptionally favourable rate. In accepting the offer, Monroe and Livingston exceeded their authority by a considerable distance. Jefferson had instructed them to inquire into possibilities and prices, not to agree to purchase. Moreover, the instruction has been issued in respect of New Orleans and Florida; no mention had been made of Louisiana. Nonetheless, Jefferson was delighted. The purchase of Louisiana was beyond his wildest dreams: it would guarantee the security of the United States and 'exclude those bickerings with foreign powers which we know of a certainty would have put us at war with France immediately; and it secures to us the course of a peaceable nation'.

However, this initial delight soon turned to consternation when Jefferson realized that not only did Monroe and

Livingston lack authority to agree to the purchase, so did he – and he lacked that authority by his own, publicly expressed, opinions and principles. For Jefferson had frequently declared that elected officials had no power to implement policies that were not granted to them by written law, and the power to purchase foreign territory was not granted to the President by written law. Nor, indeed, was it permitted by the Constitution. Since there was no time to secure an amendment to the Constitution, Jefferson authorized the purchase of Louisiana from France and thus abandoned principles which he had publicly affirmed on many occasions. Moreover, he did so for reasons of political expediency, perhaps even political necessity. In a letter written in 1810 he defended his decision in the following words:

> A strict observance of the written law is doubtless *one* of the high duties of a good citizen, but it is not *the highest*. The laws of necessity, of self-preservation, of saving our country when in danger, are of higher obligation. To lose our country by a scrupulous adherence to written law, would be to lose the law itself, with life, liberty, property and all those who are enjoying them with us; thus absurdly sacrificing the end to the means. (Jefferson, 20 September 1810, Letter to John Monticello)[2]

Jefferson's decision met with a mixed reception in his own day, but some modern commentators have had no hesitation in declaring it to be a piece of exemplary statesmanship. Thus, Newbold prefaces her discussion of the case with the following statement: 'When public servants, whether they are elected or appointed, make extraordinary decisions that elevate them to the level of statesmen despite the ethical consequences to their individual self, they are ensuring the preservation of the very

that integrity will be more difficult for politicians than for the rest of us.

Additionally, even if the appropriate limits of consequentialist thinking in politics were (somehow) known, there is a danger that those who engage in such thinking will, over time, become forgetful of the limits. Bernard Williams notes that 'only those who are reluctant or disinclined to do the morally disagreeable when it is really necessary have much chance of not doing it when it is not necessary' (Williams, 1981, p.64), and he goes on to wonder how stable this position is: those who regularly and reliably find themselves in positions where they are called upon to do what is morally disagreeable may become hardened to doing what is disagreeable. Indeed, they may, in the long run, cease to find those things disagreeable at all, and that is a worrying prospect for those of us who live under their governance.

The character of politicians

So far, I have given reasons for thinking that official roles call for increased impartiality and that political roles call for greater attention to consequences. When these are taken together, they seem to place the politician in a uniquely vulnerable position as far as integrity is concerned: impartiality undermines that part of integrity which consists in sticking by one's own values, while emphasizing consequences undermines the sense that one's own actions are a manifestation of one's values. The fact that (at least sometimes) politicians must put aside their own principles and ethical commitments in order to secure the public good can be a sign of statesmanship, but it can equally be a sign of disregard for means, and disregard for means can, in the long term, lead to callousness and ruthlessness.

Notice, moreover, that in the discussion so far, emphasis has been placed on the predictability of these situations arising. The story that has been told is not one in which, through mere bad luck, a politician finds that he must do what he believes to be wrong. On the contrary, it is a feature of politics itself that it requires attention to impartiality and to consequences, both of which are threats to integrity. But if this is the case, then questions arise both about the character of those who choose politics as a career and about the character of those who succeed in it. In the former case, we may simply note, with Williams, that a person who could not bring himself to abandon his own ethical commitments would be unsuited to a career in politics; and in the latter case we might predict that, after years of attention to consequences, the politician might cease to have any deep or serious commitments of his own. We might also wonder whether he would have become accustomed to justifying his actions in terms of their consequences and thus be more or less indifferent about the means that might be necessary to secure whatever ends were politically necessary.

All this suggests that politicians are indeed morally worse than the rest of us, but before we rush to this conclusion, it may be wise to take note of two further features of modern political life, both of which, in different ways, may serve to 'soften' that judgement. The first is that, when politicians behave badly, they may do so *for us*. It was in order to secure the prosperity and security of the United States that Jefferson exceeded his authority in purchasing Louisiana, and it was in order to secure world peace that Kennedy and Khrushchev lied and deceived in the case of the Cuban Missile Crisis.[4] One further, and final, example may help to make the point yet more starkly.

It was, until recently, widely believed that on the afternoon of 14 November 1940 Winston Churchill was informed that that night there would be a massive German air-raid on the city of Coventry. On receiving the information he could have ordered the evacuation of Coventry, but he chose not to do so and, as a result, more than 500 people (possibly as many as 1,000) died. Churchill's decision to issue no word of warning was informed by his belief that, if the Luftwaffe knew they were expected, they would draw the (correct) conclusion that British Intelligence had deciphered the German Enigma Code, and such knowledge would be disastrous for the British war effort. As with Jefferson, Truman, Kennedy, and Khrushchev, so here with Churchill, the decision was taken for and on behalf of the country as a whole. In all these cases there may well have been loss of integrity for the individuals, but in all these cases, too, there were duties – moral duties – associated with politics itself.

There is an irony here: the examples draw to our attention the fact that ruthlessness, or deceit, or a willingness to do what is morally wrong may be necessary (at least sometimes) in order to secure the good of the state, but of course these things may also be necessary in order to secure the continued success of the politician himself. Politicians who fail to secure the good of their country rapidly find themselves out of office, and it may therefore be in their own interest as politicians to lie or deceive or do wrong in the examples given. Nonetheless, the examples serve to highlight the differences between political lying and common-or-garden crookedness. The politician may indeed do what is morally wrong, but, unlike the crook, he may do that *for us*. So the conclusion that politicians are morally worse than the rest of us needs to be moderated by the recognition that we (the citizens) need people who are both able and willing to do what is morally disagreeable.

Additionally, it is important to note that typically politicians act to further the interests of their own compatriots or constituents, and this is not the same as acting so as to promote the greater good *tout court*. In other words, although politicians are required to pay increased attention to consequences, their over-riding interest is in the consequences for their own people. Thus, Churchill's duty was to promote the interests of Britain in World War II, Jefferson's duty was to promote the prosperity of the United States, and Khrushchev's duty was to secure peace for the USSR. In all these cases, concern for one's own country can lead to neglect of the interests of 'outsiders', and will license a kind of utilitarian calculation that extends only to one's own compatriots, not to humanity as a whole. This fact returns us to the possibility that, after all, politicians are morally worse than the rest of us, for in pursuing the interests of their own country and their own constituents they must, by definition, give less weight to the interests of outsiders.

The reference to 'constituents' is significant, and introduces the second feature of political life that should inform our understanding of the character of politicians. This is that politicians must act in the interests of their constituents if they are to have any serious chance of staying in power. As I have already noted, politicians who fail to secure the interests of their constituents are likely to find themselves out of office and, of course, losing office is not only damaging to the career of the politician himself, it also precludes the possibility of his realizing morally desirable outcomes. Beyond that, however, and as Michael Walzer notes:

Politicians rule over us and the pleasures of ruling are
much greater than the pleasures of being ruled. The successful politician becomes the visible architect of our
restraint. He taxes us, licenses us, forbids and permits us,
directs us to this or that distant goal – all for our greater
good. Moreover, he takes chances for our greater good that
put us, or some of us, in danger. Sometimes he puts
himself in danger too, but politics, after all, is his adven-
ture. It is not always ours. There are undoubtedly times
when it is good or necessary to direct the affairs of other
people and to put them in danger. But we are a little
frightened of the man who seeks, ordinarily and every day,
the power to do so. And the fear is reasonable enough.
The politician has, or pretends to have, a kind of confidence in his own judgement that the rest of us know to be
presumptuous in any man. (Walzer, 1974, p. 65)

The point here is that power may not simply be a necessary condition of attaining good ends, it may also be an
object of desire in itself and, when it is, it can bespeak a
kind of certainty in moral matters that is not entirely
admirable. However, here, too, we need to remember that,
even if the confidence of the politician is misplaced or
hubristic, it can also be necessary *for us* to have as our
political leaders people who lack the doubts and uncer-
tainties that assail the rest of us. Here, too, we need to
remember that the more unpleasant character traits of
politicians may be necessary if they are to do what is best
for us.

Conclusion

This chapter has focused on the question: 'Why might
integrity be more difficult for politicians than for other
people?' In responding to that question, I have noted two,

quite general, ways in which integrity may be threatened. The first arises from the fact that integrity is in tension with requirements of impartiality; the second arises from the fact that integrity is in tension with consequentialist considerations. I have noted that politics calls for a high degree of impartiality and for a heightened regard for consequences. In both these respects, therefore, it threatens to undermine integrity.

Additionally, I have raised questions about the extent to which integrity is threatened by the duties associated with official roles, and I have noted that, while all roles may require us to do things in an official capacity that we would be loath to do in a private capacity, politics appears to be especially problematic both because the politician acts (or claims to act) on our behalf and because the profession of politics is one that necessarily involves the pursuit and exercise of power over other people.

These last considerations draw our attention to questions about the kind of people we can expect to be attracted to politics, and about the qualities of character that are likely to be encouraged by a life in politics. On the former, it seems that those who are likely to want to enter politics will be, in some part, people with a very clear sense of what is right – a confidence that (as Walzer puts it) we know to be presumptuous in any man (or woman). Moreover, and because politics brings power with it, they will be people who are able and willing to call upon others to face danger, and even death, in pursuit of their principles.

However, if we think about the qualities of character that are likely to be encouraged by a life in politics, we see that rather different considerations apply. Since politics predictably gives rise to situations in which deceit, duplicity, and ruthlessness are called for, we may wonder whether the person who pursues a career in politics will eventually become inured to deceit and become a deceitful and duplicitous person. Machiavelli tells us that the politician must be willing to lie when that is necessary, but if politics predictably calls for lying, then it may be that the profession of politics will encourage a general disposition to lie.

The upshot of this discussion, therefore, is to suggest that integrity is indeed more difficult for politicians than for others. This is partly because politics demands increased attention to consequences and to impartiality, but it is also because the office of politician involves securing and exercising power over others in a realm where the politician claims to be, and often is, acting on our behalf.

In the next chapter I will examine the relationship between integrity and consequentialism in more detail. My focus will be on the claim that, although politics does indeed call for heightened attention to consequences, and although it may therefore constitute a threat to integrity, we ought not to be overly concerned about this. Integrity may be a private virtue, but it can easily translate into a public vice. So, having given reasons for thinking that integrity is indeed more difficult for politicians than the rest of us, I now turn to the question of whether we should be worried about that.

3

Integrity and Utilitarianism

> The strength of utilitarianism, the problem to which it is a truly compelling solution, is as a guide to public rather than private conduct.
>
> Goodin, 1995, p. 8

The previous chapter ended with the suggestion that one reason why integrity might be more difficult for politicians than for the rest of us is because politics calls for increased attention to consequences, and consequentialist thinking is precisely the kind of thinking that threatens integrity. The claim that consequentialist thinking threatens integrity is closely associated with Bernard Williams, and indeed is central to the critique of utilitarianism that he offers in his contribution to *Utilitarianism: For and Against*. There, he claims that moral theories which give great weight to consequences effectively make the individual a mere channel through which the plans, projects, and values of others can be realized, and in illustration of this claim he offers two very famous examples. The first example – the example of George and the job in chemical and biological warfare – has been mentioned already; the second example is the example of Jim and the Indians, which runs as follows:

Jim finds himself in the central square of a small South
American town. Tied up against the wall are a row of
Indians, most terrified, a few defiant, in front of them
several armed men in uniform. A heavy man in a sweat-
stained khaki shirt turns out to be the captain in charge
and, after a good deal of questioning of Jim which estab-
lishes that he got there by accident while on a botanical
expedition, explains that the Indians are a random group
of the inhabitants who, after recent acts of protest against
the government, are just about to be killed to remind other
possible protestors of the advantages of not protesting.
However, since Jim is an honoured visitor from another
land, the captain is happy to offer him a guest's privilege
of killing one of the Indians himself. If Jim accepts, then
as a special mark of the occasion, the other Indians will be
let off. Of course, if Jim refuses, then there is no special
occasion, and Pedro here will do what he was about to do
when Jim arrived, and kill them all. Jim, with some desper-
ate recollection of schoolboy fiction, wonders whether if
he got hold of a gun, he could hold the captain, Pedro,
and the rest of the soldiers to threat, but it is quite clear
from the set-up that nothing of that kind is going to work:
any attempt at that sort of thing will mean that all the
Indians will be killed, and himself. The men against the
wall, and the other villagers, understand the situation, and
are obviously begging him to accept. What should he do?
(Williams, 1973, pp. 98–9)

The question 'What should he do?' seems to be swiftly
answered by utilitarianism, which dictates that Jim should
do as Pedro requests, shoot one Indian, and thus save
the lives of the other nineteen. However, if Jim does
what utilitarian calculation dictates, it will be at the expense
of his own fundamental ethical commitments. The fact
that utilitarianism requires George to focus so sharply on
what will happen as a result of his action (or inaction)

rather than on what he himself does is what explains its inability to respect integrity in cases such as this, and it is that inability that is central to Williams' critique of utilitarianism.

However, if Williams takes utilitarian thinking to be potentially destructive of integrity, others have claimed that it is nonetheless exactly the sort of thinking that is both necessary and desirable in public life. In the quotation given at the head of this chapter, Robert Goodin defends utilitarianism as the appropriate decision procedure for those engaged in public policy formation, and he also notes that its founding fathers intended that its main purpose should be to inform thinking about public matters, not to act as a guide to individuals on how to conduct themselves in their ordinary, everyday lives. Moreover, Goodin is largely unconcerned about the possibility that, by engaging in utilitarian thinking, politicians will damage their integrity. This is partly because he is somewhat sceptical about the importance of integrity, and partly because he believes that a clear line can and must be drawn between the forms of thinking which are appropriate in private or personal life, on the one hand, and the forms of thinking which are appropriate when acting in a public capacity, on the other. He writes:

> Just as the special circumstances of private life are such as to drive us away from utilitarianism in any direct form, so too are the special circumstances of public life such as to drive us toward it. Those special circumstances make public life particularly conducive to the forthright application of a utilitarian doctrine. Indeed, in my view, they make it almost indecent to apply any other. (Goodin, 1995, p. 4)

So Goodin is not concerned to deny that utilitarian thinking undermines integrity; rather, he is concerned to emphasize that, even if it does undermine integrity, it is nonetheless the correct way of thinking in public life.

Is this latter claim correct? In this chapter I will discuss both the claim and its consequences for the character and integrity of politicians. However, before we can establish whether utilitarianism is indeed the correct decision procedure for those in public office, we first need to be more specific about what utilitarianism is, and about what kind of utilitarianism is being commended to those in public office. This is necessary because the discussion so far has referred not to utilitarianism in particular, but only to consequentialism in general. Recall Nagel's claim:

> Two types of concern determine the content of morality: concern with what will happen and concern with what one is doing. Insofar as principles of conduct are determined by the first consideration, they will be consequentialist, requiring that we promote the best overall results. Insofar as they are determined by the second, the influence of consequences will be limited by certain restrictions on the means to be used and by a loosening of the requirement that one always pursue the best results. (Nagel, 1978, pp. 82–3)

This, however, is too general for our purposes: both Goodin and Williams go beyond the very general thought that politics calls for increased attention to consequences, and both note that politics is closely associated with a specific kind of consequentialist thinking – namely, utilitarianism. Additionally, in commending utilitarian thinking as not only necessary but desirable in public life, Goodin emphasizes that he is speaking of a particular kind of utilitarianism – 'Government House utilitarianism'. So, in order to see the precise ways in which consequentialist thinking might (or might not) make integrity more difficult for politicians than for the rest of us, we need to nuance the discussion and examine, first, a specific form of consequentialism (utilitarianism) and then a specific form of utilitarianism (Government House utilitarianism).

From consequentialism to utilitarianism

Following Nagel, we may note, first, that consequentialist thinking emphasizes what will happen or what will promote the best overall results and, second, that utilitarianism, as a sub-set of consequentialism, offers a distinctive understanding of what will make results the best ones overall – namely, their tendency to promote happiness, or satisfaction, or (in the economists' phrase) utility. The origins of utilitarianism are to be found in two nineteenth-century thinkers, Jeremy Bentham and John Stuart Mill, both of whom commended it primarily as the correct decision procedure for public life. Robert Goodin reminds us of this when he writes: 'Whatever contemporary writers might say, "the fathers of utilitarianism thought of it principally as a system of social and political decision, as offering a criterion and basis of judgement for legislators and administrators", and this "is recognizably a different matter from utilitarianism as a system of personal morality"' (Goodin, 1995, p. 62). And he goes on to point out that Bentham spent much of his time advising on constitutional and penal reform and 'other sundry topics in public policy and administration', as did some of his immediate successors.

So the kind of consequentialism to be considered here is utilitarianism, and this is both because it is the most familiar form of consequentialism in modern moral and political philosophy, and because it is a form of consequentialism that arose, in part, as a guide to decision

making in public life. In the classical formulation offered
by John Stuart Mill, utilitarianism holds that 'actions are
right in proportion as they tend to promote happiness, and
wrong as they tend to produce the reverse of happiness.
By happiness is intended pleasure and the absence of pain;
by unhappiness, pain and the privation of pleasure' (Mill,
1978a, p. 257). In a more modern formulation it is the
moral theory that 'judges the goodness of outcomes – and
therefore the rightness of actions insofar as they affect
outcomes – by the degree to which they secure the greatest
benefit to all concerned' (Hardin as quoted in Goodin,
1995, p. 3).

Varieties of utilitarianism

The second improvement is within utilitarianism. If we
read Mill's statement (above) literally, then it seems that,
for utilitarians, decisions about what it is right to do
depend upon an assessment of the consequences that will
follow from each individual action. This form of utilitarianism (act utilitarianism) has attracted considerable criti-
cism over the years and many reasons have been adduced
to show that it is unsatisfactory or counter-intuitive. One
significant problem with this form of utilitarianism is that
it can seem to require us to do things which we know to
be unjust, simply on condition that they will produce more
benefit than any other action available to us. So, to give a
much-discussed example, act utilitarianism may demand
that we punish someone whom we know to be innocent
if that is what is needed in order to avoid civil unrest.
Discussing this possibility, E.F. Carritt writes:

> If some kind of very cruel crime becomes common, and
> none of the criminals can be caught, it might be highly

expedient, as an example, to hang an innocent man, if a charge against him could be so framed that he were universally thought guilty; indeed this would only fail to be an ideal instance of utilitarian 'punishment' because the victim himself would not have been so likely as a real felon to commit such a crime in the future; in all other respects it would be a perfect deterrent and therefore felicific. (Carritt, 1963, p. 65)

The very general point here is that act utilitarianism can require that we do things which we know to be unjust simply on condition that they produce more benefit than acting justly.

However, it is not only its tendency to commend unjust actions that makes act utilitarianism problematic. An additional, and very significant, objection to it is that it is impractical because it requires us to make vast and complex calculations about matters that are uncertain. If the right action is the action that will produce greatest welfare, or benefit, or happiness, then, in order to know what I should do in any particular case, I will need to calculate the consequences of all possible actions for all people who may be affected. This will be difficult enough in private contexts, but in political contexts, where actions may affect an entire population, or even the whole world, it will be a vast undertaking, and when that fact is combined with the fact that many political decisions have to be taken in haste, act utilitarianism appears wildly impractical as a guide to action. Commenting on this, Goodin writes that act utilitarianism 'presupposes that we are able to perform utility calculations that typically range across an enormous number of individuals and options – and that we are able to do so reliably, instantaneously, and costlessly. This is to assume away the "limits of reason" which characterize the real world for individual agents and, all the more so, for social policy-makers' (Goodin, 1995, p. 17). And he concludes that

> Often the only way to maximize the utility that arises from my act is by knowing (or guessing) what others are likely to do. But knowing that with any certainty is ...impossible (or impossibly costly) in a world populated by act-utilitarian agents. The best way to co-ordinate our actions with those of others, and thereby maximize the utility from each of our actions as individuals as well as from all of our actions collectively, is to promulgate rules (themselves chosen with an eye to maximizing utility, of course) and to adhere to them. (Goodin, 1995, p. 18)

 So it is not simply its propensity to condone unjust acts, but also the fact that it requires extensive and, in practice, impossible calculation that renders act utilitarianism both undesirable and unmanageable. In response to these problems, a number of writers, including Goodin, propose a form of utilitarianism which gives priority to rules rather than individual actions. The thought here is that, in the area of policy formation, life is too complicated to permit case-by-case decisions and therefore decisions must be taken on the basis of rules that have themselves been adopted because, if followed, they will deliver the best outcomes overall.

This move from act utilitarianism to rule utilitarianism does, however, bring problems with it. One reason for this is that rules have exceptions, and there can be cases in which breaking a rule will have better overall consequences than following it. To illustrate this, consider seat-belt legislation. We know that, as a general rule, it is safer to wear a seat-belt than not. Legislation that makes the wearing of a seat-belt compulsory is therefore justified in utilitarian terms: if followed universally, the rule will produce more benefit and less misery than a rule that prohibits the wearing of a seat-belt, or than a rule that allows freedom of choice. However, we also know that there are some – very unusual – cases in which people have been saved from death or serious injury because they were *not* wearing a seat-belt and were, for example, thrown clear of what would otherwise have been a fatal crash. In proposing that utilitarian calculation apply to rules rather than individual acts, rule utilitarians must nonetheless allow that there will be some cases in which breaking the rule will be better in terms of overall utility than following it.

The same considerations could, of course, be applied to the case of hanging an innocent man: here, too, we may acknowledge that there are some highly unusual cases, in which punishing the innocent will produce most benefit overall, but we must also acknowledge the difficulty of being sure that any particular case does indeed fall into that category and, in the case of hanging an innocent man, we must also be alert to the possibility that if it were to become widely known that innocent people would be hanged should that seem to be most beneficial, there would be considerable alarm and insecurity amongst the populace at large. And of course insecurity is itself something that exacts costs in terms of utility.

For these reasons, then, Goodin favours the adoption of rule utilitarianism in public life, where, he argues, it is both necessary and desirable: it is necessary because the area of public policy formation and implementation is, by its nature, one where averages, aggregates, and general predictions about overall outcomes are all that is available (specific and individual calculations are too complex); and it is desirable because it is a way of ensuring that the populace know what is required of them and what the penalties of non-compliance will be. Act-utilitarian calculations are not only too complex and difficult to be practical in the public realm, they will also deliver very variable and unpredictable decisions in apparently similar situations, and it is neither reasonable nor fair to expect the general public to 'second-guess' these decisions. For these reasons, then, rule utilitarianism, or what Goodin calls 'Government House utilitarianism', is to be favoured in public life. And so, Goodin concludes:

> The basic trick, to be reiterated in all such defences, is to draw a distinction between utilitarianism as a guide to personal conduct and utilitarianism as a guide to public policy-making, and to show that criticisms that are strong as applied to the former are weak as applied to the latter. What makes the claim plausible, in general, is the fact that public officials (both ought, and in any case must) govern through rules that are general in form. (Goodin, 1995, p. 77)

However, Goodin does not stop there, for he also implies that, in addition to being the appropriate decision procedure in public life, this form of utilitarianism is also much less objectionable in private life than is usually supposed. So the form of his argument is to show that Government House utilitarianism should be accepted in the public domain, that the usual objections to utilitarianism apply with much less force here than in private life, and that in fact even some of the objections to utilitarianism as a private or personal morality are less damaging than is often alleged.

Now this argumentative structure is interesting, for even if we agree with Goodin that Government House utilitarianism is both necessary and desirable in public life, that still leaves unanswered a question about the kinds of people Government House utilitarians will be. In other words, even if we allow that utilitarianism of the sort

advocated by Goodin is the appropriate decision procedure for policy makers, we might still want to know what
qualities of character will be evident in people who, as a
matter of routine, employ that decision procedure.[1] This,
of course, is a central question of this book: what kinds of
people will politicians be, and, in particular, will they be
people who have integrity in the sense outlined in Chapter
1? In the remainder of this chapter, I will address this
question and, in doing so, I will be accepting (at le _st for
the time being) that Government House utilitarianism is
an appropriate and desirable decision procedure for politicians. My focus then will be on the qualities of character
we can expect to find in politicians, so understood. Will
they be people of integrity, and, if not, is that something
which should cause us concern?

Utilitarianism and character

In previous chapters I have, by and large, been assuming
that loss of integrity is a significant and regrettable matter,
something that should concern us even if there are specific
and rather unusual cases, such as the case of Himmler, in
which we might think it better if someone had lacked
integrity. And I have also assumed (on the whole) that if
politics threatens the integrity of the politician, then that is
something which should cause us concern. However, part
of the problem which motivates this book is the problem
of saying exactly what integrity is and exactly why we
should be troubled by attacks upon it. Where integrity is
understood as a matter of standing by one's fundamental
commitments it may (as we have seen) be uncomfortably
close to stubbornness or pig-headedness or a narcissistic
concern for one's own moral purity. Additionally, where
integrity is spelled out as a matter of preserving one's true

self and remaining true to one's identity-conferring commitments, we need to be alert to the possibility that the commitments which, as a matter of fact, constitute one's sense of who one is can be quite trivial and, even if they are not, it is not clear why they should be elevated above the well-being of others. In other words, it is not clear why integrity should trump considerations of utility. Goodin expresses the point robustly when he says:

> There may well be people who are psychologically so attached to their claret club that they cannot bear to think of it being disbanded: to do so would undermine their sense of self and, with it, their very capacity for moral agency. But to say that they cannot bear to contemplate abandoning these luxuries so that others may be given the necessities of life is to say that their capacity for moral agency was pretty meagre all along. How to treat subnormals is always a tricky question. (Goodin, 1995, p. 68)

All this, however, simply confirms the point (made earlier) that integrity is not something that should always be preserved in the face of competing considerations. It does not show that integrity has no value at all, and this is crucial because Williams' complaint against utilitarianism – the complaint made manifest through the examples of George and Jim – is that it makes integrity as a value unintelligible. So, we can agree that the case of Himmler casts doubt on whether integrity is always desirable, and we can agree that there are cases in which the things that invest people's lives with meaning are fundamentally trivial – or even morally repellent – without thereby concluding that integrity is ethically unimportant or that its preservation should be (to use Goodin's terminology) a matter for confession rather than claim.

In the remainder of this chapter I want to suggest that integrity is seriously threatened by utilitarian thinking, but that the nature of the threat can best be seen not by focusing on single cases in which there is a conflict between individual integrity and the requirements of utility, but rather by focusing on the character traits which will be cultivated in those who reliably and predictably engage in the kind of Government House thinking that Goodin commends as both necessary and desirable for politicians. So my strategy is to accept the claim that politics calls for utilitarian thinking, and then go on to ask what qualities of character we might expect in a person who, for many years, has engaged in such thinking. To anticipate, my conclusion will be that for such a person, integrity will prove to be incomprehensible rather than difficult, and that there are two reasons why that is so – reasons of psychology and reasons of phenomenology.

Reasons of psychology

Consider, first, the politician or policy maker who, following Goodin's advice, adopts rule-utilitarian reasoning when formulating policy and introducing legislation. As a utilitarian he believes that the right thing to do is the thing that will produce best overall results, and as a policy maker he knows that he cannot consider actions on a case-by-case basis: there is not enough time to do so, he lacks sufficient information to enable him to do so, and in any case, doing so would leave the general public unsure about what is required of them. In a perfect world, and with perfect information, he would presumably adopt act-utilitarian reasoning, but he is not in a perfect world and he therefore adopts rule-utilitarian thinking. Suppose, however, that in a specific case he sees very clearly that following the rule will result in less overall benefit than breaking it. What should he do? If he breaks the rule and is known to do so, then of course he ceases to be reliable in the way politicians should be, but, assuming either that he can preserve secrecy or that the costs of adverse publicity are factored in to his calculations, he will still be producing greater overall benefit if, on this occasion, he breaks the rule. Or so we may suppose. On the other hand, if he keeps the rule, then he will be doing so in disregard of the reasons he had for adopting it in the first place. So all the utilitarian reasons seem, on this occasion, to speak in favour of breaking the rule.

To see what is at stake here, consider again the case of hanging the innocent man. As standardly told, the situation is this: we adopt a general rule of punishing all and only those who are guilty. The rule is adopted because, in general, it produces greater benefit than any other rule and the benefit it produces includes the benefit of enabling the populace to feel secure: because the rule is in place, they know that they will not be punished simply in order to quieten an unruly and lawless rabble. However, the considerations that govern the adoption of the rule do not apply in the specific case envisaged by Carritt, for here following the rule (punish only the guilty) will produce less benefit than breaking it.

Now normally, this kind of example is introduced as a way of showing that rule utilitarianism collapses into act utilitarianism, and that act utilitarianism is unacceptable because it delivers unjust decisions in specific cases. However, that is not the objection I wish to press here. My concern is not with the justice of the decision to hang the innocent man, but with the character of the person who takes that decision. There are two stages to the discussion. First, we can ask how such a man is to think of his own act. Commenting on this, Bernard Williams writes:

We need to hold on to the idea, and to find politicians who hold on to the idea, that there are actions which remain morally disagreeable even when politically justified. The point of this is not at all that it is unedifying to have politicians who, while as ruthless in action as others, are unhappy about it. Sackcloth is not suitable dress for politicians, least of all successful ones. The point is that only those who are reluctant or disinclined to do the morally disagreeable when it is really necessary will have much chance of not doing it when it is not necessary. (Williams, 1981, p. 62)

The crucial thought here is that there can be actions (hanging the innocent man, for example) which are politically necessary but which most of us would find morally disagreeable. For the thoroughgoing, or act, utilitarian, however, the thought that this act is morally disagreeable is not fully available. As a utilitarian, he believes that the right act is the act that will produce more benefit than any other. If hanging the innocent man is indeed, and in this case, the act that will produce more benefit (and avert more harm) than any other, then it is the right act and the act he should perform. The thought that it is morally disagreeable is incoherent from a utilitarian point of view, for what could moral disagreeableness be if, as here, the act is the best one in utilitarian terms? Williams refers to the difficulty of ensuring that a person will be willing to do what is morally disagreeable when it is necessary, but not when it is not necessary, but this point disguises a deeper one, which is that, from a utilitarian point of view, it is hard to see how anything could be morally disagreeable if it is justified in utilitarian terms. This consideration leads to a second, which involves a move from act utilitarianism to rule utilitarianism and a move from questions of psychology to questions of phenomenology.

where I am convinced that breaking the rule will promote the best outcome, but if it will promote the best outcome, why should I feel reluctant in advance or feel guilty with hindsight? This form of utilitarianism can explain and justify hesitancy – since my calculations may be wrong or my predictions uncertain – but it cannot explain reluctance or guilt understood as distinctively *moral* sentiments. And what we expect people to feel when faced with the prospect of breaking a well-established, and justifiable, rule is a sense that they are doing (or have done) something morally wrong.

In short, then, the allegation here is that utilitarianism is phenomenologically defective, since it has no way of explaining the agent's sense that he or she has done something morally wrong in breaking a rule. More generally, the claim is that, since utilitarianism takes moral rightness to be determinable along a single dimension (benefit and harm), it has no way of explaining how an agent might come to feel that moral cost attaches to particular actions even though those actions are ones that deliver greatest benefit and least harm. But the sense that something is morally costly, even though it delivers most benefit, is a familiar one, and so (the argument goes) any theory that cannot explain this familiar feeling is, to that extent, phenomenologically defective.

Both the preceding arguments – the argument from psychology and the argument from phenomenology – point to utilitarianism's inability to explain sentiments which are familiar and which, intuitively, we believe to be rational, appropriate, and desirable. They thereby raise questions about the kind of people thoroughgoing utilitarians would be. For instance, they prompt us to ask what sort of person would be capable of hanging an innocent man while feeling no reluctance, regret, or remorse – even in circumstances where doing so would be 'for the best' all round. And they suggest that, even if utilitarianism is indeed the best decision procedure for policy makers, it is also a decision procedure that could be followed reliably only by people who either lacked normal psychological responses or would come to have abnormal psychological responses after a period of time spent in politics. Politics selects for ruthlessness, and utilitarianism cultivates ruthlessness.

Conclusion

Politics, it is said, is a matter of getting results, and therefore those who enter the profession of politics must be prepared to place greater emphasis on what happens as a result of what they do than on what they do. Politics calls for consequentialist thinking, and the best form of consequentialist thinking to adopt in political life is a form of rule utilitarianism. The reasons for this are: first, and from the point of view of the public official or policy maker, applying a rule which has been adopted because of its general tendency to produce better results is the most appropriate way of responding to complex circumstances in which information is only partial; second, and from the point of view of the populace (or those who are subject to the rules), rule utilitarianism offers reliability and transparency. People know why the rules have been selected, they know what those rules require of them, and they know that the rules will be reliably applied and enforced.

Against this, however, it has been suggested that, even if there are powerful reasons for thinking that rule utilitarianism is the best and most appropriate way of making decisions in public life, there are also reasons for being glad that not everyone is able to bring themselves to behave in accordance with it. The reasons for this are: first, that insofar as utilitarian thinking cannot render coherent the tendency to feel reluctance or regret in cases such as that of hanging, or shooting, the innocent man, it promotes callousness and disregard of others; and, second, the best way to promote the greatest happiness may not be to pursue a policy or follow a set of rules designed to promote the greatest happiness. The former reason suggests that those who are thoroughgoing utilitarians will be morally vacuous; the latter suggests that they will not necessarily be successful even in their utilitarian aims.

My overall purpose in this book is to assess the familiar claim that there is a tension between morality and politics. In particular, it is to assess the claim that politics undermines integrity, where that claim arises from two thoughts: first, that politics demands utilitarian thinking; and, second, that utilitarian thinking undermines integrity. If it is true that politics requires utilitarian thinking, and if it is also true that utilitarian thinking undermines integrity, then it seems to follow that politics undermines integrity. However, the considerations offered here do not suggest simply that politics threatens integrity; they suggest that the kind of thinking required by politics makes integrity as a value incomprehensible or incoherent. So the truly successful politician will not find his integrity undermined by political life, since he will have no integrity to be undermined. In a passage quoted earlier, Michael Walzer says that it is by his dirty hands that we know the moral politician: 'If he were a moral man and nothing else, his hands would not be dirty; if he were a politician and nothing else, he would pretend that they were clean' (Walzer, 1974, p. 70).

Walzer's proviso suggests that utilitarianism does not give a satisfactory answer to our initial question. It explains why the politician may be ruthless, but it does not (and arguably cannot) explain why he will be reluctant, regretful, or guilty about the difficult things he has to do. Indeed, if he is a consistent utilitarian, he will not see these things as problematic in the first place and, to that extent, he will lack integrity entirely rather than being someone for whom the profession of politics undermines integrity.

If, then, we want an account of how integrity may be threatened by politics, we need to look elsewhere, for utilitarianism does not so much jeopardize integrity as render it unintelligible. In the next two chapters I will discuss two further ways in which the tension between integrity and politics may be explained. The first involves appeal to value pluralism; the second involves appeal to social roles.

4

Integrity and Pluralism

[T]here are at least two worlds: each of them has much, indeed everything, to be said for it; but they are two and not one. One must learn to choose between them and, having chosen, not look back.

Berlin, 1992, p. 218

The conviction that there is a deep, and possibly ineradicable, tension between politics and morality is most closely associated with Machiavelli. Indeed, Machiavelli's name has entered the English language as a byword for political duplicity, ruthlessness, and immorality. The *Concise Oxford English Dictionary* defines 'machiavellian' as 'elaborately cunning; scheming, unscrupulous', and goes on to refer to Machiavelli as someone who 'advocated resort to morally questionable methods in the interests of the State'. By common consent, it is Machiavelli who tells us that in politics the end justifies the means and that politicians must be prepared to do evil that good may come. He is the original, and supreme, proponent of realism in politics, and the most articulate champion of the truth that, in politics, moral goodness must bend the knee to political expediency. Or is he?

In a famous essay entitled 'The Question of Machiavelli', Isaiah Berlin notes the discomfiture which Machiavelli's pronouncements have caused through the ages and the plethora of interpretations of his writings. He argues that this vast number and range of interpretations cannot adequately be explained by appeal to Machiavelli's realism, or his advocacy of brutal and unscrupulous means in politics, since neither is unique to or distinctive of him. Thus Berlin writes, 'The fact that the wicked are seen to flourish or that wicked courses appear to pay has never been very remote from the consciousness of mankind' (Berlin, 1992, p. 207), and he goes on to cite the Bible, Herodotus, Thucydides, Plato, Aristotle, and many others in support of that claim. So, for Berlin, the common perception of Machiavelli as the gangsters' friend, as Old Nick, or as the advocate of means–end rationality is simply inadequate to explain either the variety of interpretations that have been offered of his work, or their persistent and continuing ability to shock.

What, then, is the explanation of this phenomenon? As the quotation at the head of this chapter suggests, what Berlin finds disturbing (*erschreckend*, to use his own word) about Machiavelli is that he countenances the possibility of there being more than one set of values, and he countenances the further possibility that these different sets of values may be incompatible with one another. On this interpretation, Machiavelli does not believe that the politician acts instrumentally, or that he is someone who is willing to sacrifice morality to efficiency. On the contrary, he believes that the politician positively embraces morality, but that his morality is quite different from, and indeed in conflict with, ordinary, in this case Christian, morality. His morality is the morality of politics itself. As Berlin puts it, '[T]here are at least two worlds: each of them has much, indeed everything, to be said for it; but they are two and not one. One must learn to choose between them and, having chosen, not look back.' And he goes on to insist that it is this pluralism about value which explains both the endless debates about Machiavelli's views and the *erschreckend* character of his thought, for value pluralism presents us with the possibility that the politician who acts ruthlessly and duplicitously is not immoral or amoral, but a completely consistent and wholehearted proponent of a quite different set of values. And if this is the case, then his ruthlessness and duplicity may be entirely compatible with integrity. It is this that is the truly terrifying possibility.

This chapter will be devoted to an examination of pluralism and of its implications for the possibility of moral goodness in politics. In discussing these issues, I will proceed in three stages: first, I will say something about what pluralism is, and about the different kinds of pluralism that are invoked in moral and political philosophy; then I will consider the reasons why the possibility of pluralism is *erschreckend* before finally going on to discuss the implications of pluralism for politics in general and for the moral character of politicians in particular. I begin, then, with a discussion of pluralism.

Pluralism

Although pluralism takes many forms, the important kind of pluralism for the purposes of this chapter, and indeed for this book as a whole, is the value pluralism identified by Isaiah Berlin in 'The Question of Machiavelli' and endorsed by him both in that article and in his writings more generally.[1] This kind of pluralism denies that there is a single, correct set of moral values and argues instead that there are many sets of moral values, not all of which are compatible with one another. The literature on pluralism is vast and complex, but for my purposes here the crucial point can be stated briefly, and it is this: in asking whether politics is compatible with moral goodness (whether politicians can be morally good), we assume that there is a single thing – moral goodness – and we then go on to wonder to what extent the demands of politics are compatible with the demands of that single thing, moral goodness. But why do we believe that moral goodness is unitary? Might it not be the case that there are different kinds of goodness – different kinds of value – and that the values endorsed and displayed by the politician are values which are every bit as important and valuable as conventional moral values, even though they are inconsistent with them?

The suggestion that is being canvassed here can be considered in two stages: first, it is possible that there are different sets of value; and, second, it is possible that amongst those different kinds of value will be the values of politics itself. To take the first possibility first, why might we think that there are different sets of values? Consider the following extract from a book on humility:

> Aquinas warns us that what he calls 'earthly things' have the power to enthrall us, drawing us away from the contemplative and worshipful life we ought to lead, and thus are better put aside. Ignatius Loyola puts it more powerfully, as usual: I should 'ask for understanding of the world so that I may hate it, and put away from me worldly and vain things'. The life we ought to lead, on this view, is to praise, reverence and serve God. We need very little by way of material goods in order to manage this. We would know as much, if we understood ourselves and our place in the scheme of things, and we would do our best to stop even wanting more than the minimum.... Since we are to model ourselves after Jesus, rather than pridefully seeking to live in some different way of our own design, we are to live simply as well. (Richards, 1992, p. 168)

We can see from this quotation that the values which are being commended by Aquinas and Ignatius Loyola are values associated with a life of simplicity, of unworldliness, and of obedience to God. They give high priority to domesticity, to private life rather than public life; and they place great store by the virtues of humility, self-denial, and obedience. Similarly, consider the following description of the Old Order Amish:

> The size and number of mirrors in a society indicate the cultural importance attached to the self. Thus it is not surprising that the mirrors found in Amish houses are smaller and fewer than those found in modern ones. Whereas Moderns are preoccupied with 'finding themselves', the Amish are engaged in 'losing themselves'. The Amish work just as hard at losing themselves as Moderns work at finding themselves. (Richards, 1992, p. 181)

Both quotations describe societies with distinctive understandings of what the good life consists in. Moreover, both quotations enable us to see that what counts as valuable or virtuous in one society may be of marginal value or of no value at all in another society. We are told that the Amish work as hard at losing themselves as we work at finding ourselves, and it is implicit in this that the kind of concern for autonomy and self-discovery that often dominates modern life is of no significance in Amish life. Indeed, for the Amish, paying attention to self-discovery would be considered a vice, not a virtue at all.

But if we moderns extol the virtues of a life of self-discovery, and if the Old Order Amish extol the virtues of a life of quiet contemplation, the ancient Greeks emphasized the values of citizenship and of public duty. Here is a section from Thucydides' *Peloponnesian War* in which Pericles salutes those who have died in battle:

Such was the end of these men; they were worthy of Athens, and the living need not desire to have a more heroic spirit, although they may pray for a less fatal issue. The value of such a spirit is not to be expressed in words. Any one can discourse to you for ever about the advantages of a brave defense, which you know already. But instead of listening to him I would have you day by day fix your eyes upon the greatness of Athens, until you become filled with the love of her; and when you are impressed by the spectacle of her glory, reflect that this empire has been acquired by men who knew their duty and had the courage to do it, who in the hour of conflict had the fear of dishonor always present to them, and who, if ever they failed in an enterprise, would not allow their virtues to be lost to their country, but freely gave their lives to her as the fairest offering which they could present at her feast. The sacrifice which they collectively made was individually repaid to them; for they received again each one for himself a praise which grows not old, and the noblest of all tombs, I speak not of that in which their remains are laid, but of that in which their glory survives, and is proclaimed always and on every fitting occasion both in word and deed. For the whole earth is the tomb of famous men; not only are they commemorated by columns and inscriptions in their own country, but in foreign lands there dwells also an unwritten memorial of them, graven not on stone but in the hearts of men. Make them your examples, and, esteeming courage to be freedom and freedom to be happiness, do not weigh too nicely the perils of war....To a man of spirit, cowardice and disaster coming together are far more bitter than death striking him unperceived at a time when he is full of courage and animated by the general hope. (Thucydides, *Peloponnesian War*, Book II, Section 43)[2]

The values that are commended by Pericles are values of citizenship and of public service; the primary virtue is the virtue of courage in battle, and the most important duty of each man is not to turn away from the world, but to 'fix his eyes upon the greatness of Athens'. Where the Amish commend simplicity, obedience, and unworldliness, Pericles urges men to focus their attention on the flourishing of the city state and to cultivate those virtues which will enable their city to become great. Each kind of life – the life of members of the Old Order Amish and the life of citizens in Periclean Athens – contains much that is valuable, but the two ethical worlds are incompatible with one another and it is impossible for someone to lead a life which displays the virtues of both worlds in equal measure.

Politics and pluralism

Why, though, is this *erschreckend*? The possibility which Berlin identifies and which he believes to provide the explanation of Machiavelli's continuing ability to disturb is the possibility that politics is a world of value distinct from the world of conventional, Christian, morality and indeed incompatible with it, yet nonetheless a world which makes demands that are both ultimate and compelling. So whereas modern writers believe that politicians abandon morality in order to do what is politically necessary or expedient, Machiavelli believes that politicians embrace, or may embrace, a different set of values entirely – the values of politics itself. In acting duplicitously, ruthlessly, and murderously, they do not sacrifice moral goodness to political necessity, or indeed to anything. On the contrary, they obey dutifully and absolutely the imperatives of their chosen world – the world of politics. Here is Berlin's description of the situation:

> His [Machiavelli's] vision is social and political. Hence the traditional view of him as simply a specialist in how to get

the better of others, a vulgar cynic who says that Sunday School precepts are all very well, but in a world full of evil men, a man must lie, kill, and betray if he is to get somewhere is incorrect. The philosophy summarized by 'eat or be eaten, beat or be beaten'...is not what is central to him. Machiavelli is not especially concerned with the opportunism of ambitious individuals; the ideal before his eyes is a shining vision of Florence or of Italy. (Berlin, 1992, p. 216)

And again:

Machiavelli's views, I should like to repeat, are not instrumental, but moral and ultimate, and he calls for great sacrifices in their name. For them he rejects the rival scale – the Christian principles of *ozio* [piety] and meekness, not, indeed, as being defective in themselves, but as inapplicable to the conditions of real life; and real life for him means not merely (as is sometimes alleged) life as it was lived around him in Italy – the crimes, hypocrisies, brutalities, follies of Florence, Rome, Venice, Milan. This is not the touchstone of reality. His purpose is not to leave unchanged or to reproduce this kind of life, but to lift it to a new plane, to rescue Italy from squalor and slavery, to restore her to health and sanity. (p. 216)

For Machiavelli, then, the task of establishing and nurturing the state is of cardinal importance, and it follows that the man who chooses the political life, whose vision is a 'shining vision' of Florence or of Italy, is not a man without morality, but a man with a very distinctive and demanding morality – the morality of politics itself. So Berlin notes, first, the possibility of pluralism – the possibility that there is more than one set of values and that the different sets may not be compatible with one another; and he then goes on to suggest that politics itself is a world of value and that it calls for ruthlessness, duplicity, and brutality. In the world of politics, Berlin suggests, ruthlessness and duplicity are ultimate values and they are not vices, but virtues. Given the modern tendency to read Machiavelli as an instrumentalist or realist writer, it is worth explaining Berlin's claim in a little more detail.

In his book *Innocence and Experience*, Stuart Hampshire adopts something very like Berlin's interpretation of Machiavelli when offering an explanation of how there can be different and conflicting, yet equally valuable, ways of life. Hampshire describes these different ways in terms of a conflict between innocence and experience, and he notes that

> Machiavelli himself is an advocate of one specific conception of the good, a conception that is far more widespread and influential than is generally acknowledged in books on moral philosophy. The human good in this conception consists in glorious worldly achievements which will be recognised in history: everyone ought to aspire to some form of memorable greatness, as far as he or she can. The most evident form of greatness is supreme political power, the power of the successful statesman. (Hampshire, 1992, p. 165)

And again:

> Machiavelli's problem, the conflict between personal honour and public responsibility, has only a complicated answer, at least on a philosophical level. First must come a concession to Machiavelli: in general, it is true that moral innocence and purity are incompatible with the effective exercise of political power on any considerable scale, and that two conceptions of virtue and of responsible action, attached to two very different ways of life, have to be recognised; and they have to be recognised as

a duality that persists through all periods of history....The virtues of innocence, which are not necessarily the 'monkish virtues', realise conceptions of the good which can inspire strong emotions and great admiration: absolute integrity, gentleness, disposition to sympathy, a fastidious sense of honour, generosity, a disposition to gratitude. The virtues of experience can equally inspire strong emotions and great admiration: tenacity and resolution, courage in the face of risk, intelligence, largeness of design and purpose, exceptional energy, habit of leadership. (p. 177)

The thought that dominates here is that, rather than assuming that goodness operates across one dimension and then asking how each person, whether schoolteacher or Amish or philosopher or politician, is to be ranked along that dimension, we should instead recognize that different ways of life reflect different values and call for different, and possibly incompatible, virtues. The life of innocence (as Hampshire calls it) which is led by the members of the Old Order Amish is a life that gives centrality to virtues such as humility and obedience. By contrast, the life of a statesman in Renaissance Florence is one in which humility and obedience can have no prominent place, not least because a statesman who displays these qualities will almost certainly fail to promote the best interests of the state, but instead will preside over its downfall. Politics calls for courage, daring, boldness, and audacity. Insofar as Amish life rejects these qualities and denies their status as virtues, it is a life that is incompatible with politics, and it might even be said that the Amish virtues of obedience and self-abnegation are positive vices when displayed by those who occupy political or public positions.

Commenting on Quaker life, which he uses as the paradigm case of a life of innocence, Hampshire says, 'The

Quaker conception of the good life is necessarily an innocent life, uncontaminated by violence and deceit and luxury, and by the complex and unclean calculations that support violence and deceit and luxury' (p. 173). By contrast:

> In chancelleries and palaces, and in the corridors of power, ideals of personal integrity and of moral innocence are kept in abeyance. An over-riding loyalty is owed to an institution of which one is a part or to a political cause which one believes to be substantially just...persons having this conception of the good are not subverters of all morality. They have a distinct and defensible notion of moral responsibility. (p. 175)

Hampshire's contrast between innocence and experience echoes Berlin's interpretation of Machiavelli according to which 'there are at least two worlds of value: each of them has much, indeed everything, to be said for it; but they are two and not one'. So, on this account, it is a mistake to judge the world of politics, or the life of a politician, against an allegedly overarching moral scale. It is a mistake to ask, as I have been doing throughout this book, 'Can politicians be morally good?', since this question assumes what is not true – namely, that there is a single standard of moral goodness against which all can be assessed.

The important point to be noted here is that since it is impossible to reconcile all values, when we decide in favour of one world and against another it is certain that we will lose something of value. In choosing the life of religious obedience, one forfeits the possibility of cultivating the virtues associated with the life of politics, and vice versa. There is no single right way of living, and, as Hampshire concludes:

A philosopher in his study is in no position to lay down rules for justified murders and reasonable treachery. Nor can one determine *a priori* what degree of achievement outweighs what degrees of inhumanity in the means employed. Once again the philosophical point to be recorded is that there is no completeness and no perfection to be found in morality. (p. 177)

Consequences of pluralism

But if all this is true, what are the implications for political integrity? How does the recognition that values are plural, conflicting, yet also ultimate affect our understanding of the possibility of politicians being morally good? In some part, and as foreshadowed, value pluralism answers these questions by rejecting their assumptions. In particular, it denies the assumption that moral goodness is a single thing and insists instead that value comes in many forms, not all of which are consistent one with another. So, when someone chooses the life of politics, he or she chooses a specific set of values and aspires to a specific set of virtues which are, certainly, virtues, but which are not compatible with the virtues associated with other kinds of life, such as a life of religious obedience, or a 'life of the mind'. Since values are plural and not always harmoniously reconcilable with one another, there will not be a single kind of life that is best or most valuable *tout court*.

Beyond that, however, Berlin himself suggests two implications of value pluralism, both of which are instructive for the central questions of this book. The first, and apparently negative, implication is that, since there is no single right answer to the question of how one should live, the possibility of tragedy is permanent. On this, he writes:

> Machiavelli's cardinal achievement is the uncovering of an insoluble dilemma, the planting of a permanent question mark in the path of posterity. It stems from his *de facto* recognition that ends equally ultimate, equally sacred, may contradict each other; that entire systems of value may come into collision without possibility of rational arbitration, and that not merely in exceptional circumstances, as a result of abnormality or accident, or error, but as part of the normal human situation. (Berlin, 1992, pp. 231–2)

Note here Berlin's comment that the possibility of a collision of values is 'part of the normal human situation'. It is an implication of this claim that the condition of the politician is, in fact, the human condition. Because values conflict and because they cannot all be harmoniously reconciled, we may all be confronted by a choice between goods that are equally valuable, equally ultimate; and we may all find that there is no rational way of choosing between those different sets of values or of ranking them on a single scale. When this happens, we face choices that are at best difficult and at worst tragic. This latter claim needs some explanation, not least because there are some important differences between cases that call for tragic choices and cases of dirty hands.

So far, I have followed Michael Walzer in referring to the case of the politician who is required to do something he believes to be morally wrong as a case of 'dirty hands'. Such cases are, Walzer says, cases in which:

> We know that he [the politician] is doing right when he makes the deal because he knows that he is doing wrong. I don't mean merely that he will feel badly, or even very badly, after he makes the deal. If he is the good man I am imagining him to be, he will feel guilty, that is, he will believe himself to be guilty. That is what it means to have dirty hands. (Walzer, 1974, p. 68)

What is crucial here, and what I have emphasized throughout, is the fact that dirty hands cases are characterized as cases in which it is (somehow) right to do wrong. And then, of course, the question is: 'How can it be right to do what is wrong?'

Value pluralism responds to the problem of dirty hands by undermining the assumptions on which it operates. In particular, value pluralism denies that there is some one thing which is right but which must be forgone in certain circumstances. Rather, it insists that often there are several 'right' things depending on who one is and the set of values one embraces: so, what is right for the politician whose eyes are set on a shining vision of Florence is not right for the priest whose eyes are set on obedience to God and on salvation in eternity. But – emphatically – creating and sustaining the shining vision that is Florence is just as valuable as obeying God (this – to repeat – is the *erschreck-end* implication of pluralism).

However, although the question of what it is good to do depends on the set of values and virtues one has embraced, there may, in the end, be no rational way of deciding which set of values one should embrace, and this is because the diverse and conflicting values are, to recall, 'equally ultimate, equally sacred'. It follows, then, that any single life will be one which lacks or even denies some values, and it also follows that the choice between values may be 'tragic' just in the sense that, whatever one does, something valuable will have been lost. So, whereas dirty hands cases, as characterized by Walzer and others, are cases in which one has to do wrong in order to do right, tragic choice cases are ones in which there is no right thing to do. Whatever one does is wrong.

To see the difference between dirty hands cases and tragic choice cases, consider the eponymous heroine of William Styron's novel *Sophie's Choice* (1979). Sophie is

a Polish survivor of Auschwitz and the 'choice' which is
presented to her shortly after her arrival there is the
choice as to which of her twin children shall be gassed
immediately and which shall be spared. She chooses to
condemn her daughter, Eva, to death, and for the rest of
her life she lives with the guilt that is attendant on that
decision. Whereas Walzer's politician has dirty hands
because he has had to do wrong in order to do right, for
Sophie there was no right thing to do. There was only
the 'choice' between different, equally wrong, things.
And it is in this that the tragedy of her situation lies.

Reading this back onto the case of the politician, we
can now see that where someone has wholeheartedly
embraced a set of values, the possibility of tragedy recedes
and this is because wholehearted commitment to a set of
values means that the choice has already been made. He
simply does what the values of his world dictate. Thus,
'To be a physician is to be a professional, ready to burn,
to cauterize, to amputate; if that is what the disease
requires, then to stop halfway because of personal qualms,
or some rule unrelated to your art and its technique, is a
sign of muddle and weakness and will always give you the
worst of both worlds' (Berlin, 1992, p. 218). So, for the
man who is genuinely committed, there is no anguish, no
guilt, and no tragedy. 'His own withers', as Berlin puts it,
'are unwrung' (p. 229). Anguish, guilt, and tragedy are
the preserve of the person who sees both worlds and cannot
(yet) decide between them, or commit wholeheartedly to
one of them, but what is *erschreckend* about Machiavelli's
politician is precisely that he has committed wholeheartedly to the 'shining vision' of a flourishing state and is
prepared to do whatever is necessary in order to secure
that ideal. What is *erschrekend* about him is that he does
not recognize moral conflict or the possibility of tragedy.
He has chosen, and, having chosen, he does not look back.

However, having drawn attention to the connection between pluralism and tragedy, Berlin goes on to note a second and more positive implication of pluralism. This is that the recognition of value pluralism may make possible toleration and compromise. In a line of thought that reverberates throughout his writings he speaks of the evil that is consequent upon the belief that '[s]omewhere in the past or the future, in this world or the next, in the church or the laboratory, in the speculations of the metaphysicians, in the findings of the social scientists, or in the uncorrupted heart of the simple, good man, there is to be found the final solution of the question of how men should live' (Berlin, 1969, p. 167). And it is a concomitant of this thought that pluralism, understood as the belief that values are many and not one, will lead to greater toleration of diversity. It is also a concomitant of this thought that the politician is not in a different position from all the rest of us. The need to choose between ends that are equally sacred and equally ultimate is something that will (or at least can) affect us all, and, to that extent, the conflict between morality and politics is but one manifestation of a more general conflict between different value sets. To put the point straightforwardly, then, if values are plural and conflicting, we are all likely to find, at some time in our lives, that we need to choose between them and that there is not (or need not be) any rational way of choosing. I may, for example, be faced with a choice between looking after an infirm mother and executing my professional duties as a teacher. The values required in order to be a good daughter are not the same as the values required to be a good teacher, and it may be that I am forced to choose between them. Such choices can be tragic and are to be distinguished from dirty hands cases for the latter are cases in which there is something which is right overall, but doing that right thing involves dong what is wrong. In tragic cases, by contrast, there is no right thing overall and the tragedy arises from the very recognition that, whatever values one chooses, one has sacrificed something of equal value.

Conclusion

The discussion of value pluralism raises the possibility that tensions between morality and politics may be best understood as tensions between different sets of values none of which is uniquely 'moral' and not all of which are harmoniously reconcilable. If this is indeed the case, then two things follow for an assessment of the relationship between morality and the profession of politics. The first is that the politician may not be a man who sacrifices morality to expediency. Of course, he can be that, but he need not be. He may instead be someone whose values are the values of politics itself, and if this is so, then politics does not undermine his integrity, for the politician who embraces the values of politics and, as Berlin puts it, 'does not look back', retains integrity – the integrity that is consequent upon sticking by the values of politics itself.[3]

The second implication is that politics need not be a special case. On the contrary, if value pluralism is true, then conflicts of values, and the need to choose between different sets of values, is part of the normal human condition from which none of us is, in principle, exempt, and this can be seen very clearly when we consider the fact that to be a politician is to occupy one social role amongst others. We all occupy social roles, and we may all find that those social roles (mother, daughter, teacher, lawyer, priest) make demands on us that are at odds with one another and with what we might antecedently consider morally right. When that happens, we, too, will need to decide which values are the ones we embrace and which ones are definitive of our lives. As Charles Taylor has put it:

> [E]ven if we see a plurality of final ends of equal rank, we still have to *live* them; that is, we have to design a life in which they can somehow be integrated, in some proportions, since any life is finite and cannot admit of unlimited pursuit of any good. The sense of a life – or design or plan, if we want to emphasize our powers of leading here – is necessarily one. (Taylor, 1997, p. 183)

The problem, then, is this: even if, as Berlin insists, values are plural, ultimate, and conflicting, life is single, and therefore we must, somehow, reconcile the conflicting demands made on us by the different roles we play in our lives. To be a politician of the kind described by Machiavelli is to embrace one set of values (one world) wholeheartedly and, if one is able to do that, then there is no conflict, no tragedy, no loss of or even threat to integrity. If, however, one recognizes different and conflicting values, then the preservation of integrity is more difficult and the possibility of tragic loss is permanent. These considerations bring us now, and finally, to the possibility that integrity is not undermined by consequentialism, nor by pluralism, but by the fact that we occupy many different and conflicting social roles. It is this possibility which will form the basis of discussion in the next, and final, chapter.

somehow, navigate our way between the many different
and conflicting demands that are made upon us and
through the different and conflicting values that those
demands often reflect. Moreover, having done this, we
must emerge with a single life that is coherent and has
integrity.

The aim of this chapter, then, is to investigate the relationship between integrity and social role. Of course, the
most significant social role for my purposes is the role
of politician, and the most significant question for this
book is whether holding political office is compatible
with moral goodness, but the arguments of the previous
chapter have served to suggest that, insofar as values are
irreducibly plural, it is not only politicians, but all of us
who must confront the possibility that our most fundamental values may conflict with the values embedded in
and demanded by the social roles we occupy. Put differently, if integrity is a matter of standing by one's most
fundamental ethical commitments, then the danger that
those commitments will conflict with the duties of office
is a danger which each and every one of us may well
confront.

In this chapter I will look at the ways in which the
obligations associated with social roles may make demands
upon us, and I will also consider the ways in which
we may understand our relationship to our social roles
or professional obligations. If Machiavelli's politician is
alarming because he is nothing more or other than his
role, then we need to explain what the proper balance
between self and role is both for politicians and for the
rest of us (since we all have social roles). However,
expressing the problem in this way is both revealing and
(possibly) misleading, for it supposes that there is, so to
speak, a 'self' which lies beneath the social roles. It supposes that, in addition to being a daughter, a teacher, a

wife, there is also someone who I am – the essential *me* – and that integrity is a matter of being true to the essential me. It is, as has repeatedly been emphasized, a matter of standing by my most fundamental ethical commitments. However, we are now in a position to see that this way of understanding integrity, and indeed of understanding the relationship between a person and his or her social roles, is both contentious and culturally specific. In an article entitled 'Of Masks and Men', Martin Hollis notes that questions of integrity, of dirty hands, and of tragic choices occur most frequently in ancient Greek tragedy. Indeed, one of the main points of Greek tragedy is to draw our attention to the fact that there can be cases in which we stand under conflicting, yet equally important, obligations. As an example of this, consider the case of Sophocles' Antigone. Hollis writes:

> Antigone must decide whether to bury her brother, Poly-nices, who lies dead outside the walls of Thebes after his treasonous attack on the city. Family duty commands burial, but she is also subject to the King's edict forbidding burial for a traitor. The king is Kreon and his edict embodies hallowed custom, but he is also her uncle, head of her house, and bound by family duty. Antigone decides to follow what she takes to be the higher law and buries her brother; Kreon does what he takes to be his greater duty and has her walled up alive. (Hollis, 1996, p. 98)

Now one, intuitively appealing, way of understanding the case of Antigone is to say that, although she stands under conflicting duties, in the end she decides to follow her conscience. She stands by her most fundamental ethical commitments and thus preserves her integrity. However, it may be said that this is a rather anachronistic way of understanding the situation, and that it is so because, unlike us moderns, characters in Greek tragedy are entirely specified by their social roles. In Greek tragedy, the actors appear masked, and one important purpose of the masks is to emphasize the supreme importance of social role. To the extent that this is so, there is nothing which Antigone should do *as an individual* or *as herself*. There are only the things she ought to do given the social roles she occupies – the roles of sister and of citizen. On this account, then, her tragedy lies precisely in the fact that what she ought to do as a sister (bury her brother) conflicts with what she ought to do as a citizen (obey the King). To put the point provocatively, what is sometimes said or implied about Greek tragedy is that it gains its tragic nature precisely from the fact that there was, for the Greeks, no individual – no self lying beneath, or rising above, social roles, and therefore conflicts between different social roles were insoluble (see Hollis, 1996, p. 104).

However, and as the story goes, the situation is different for us moderns because we have not only different and conflicting social roles, but also a sense of who we are independent of and antecedent to those social roles. Indeed, and as has been emphasized, integrity, understood as standing by one's most fundamental ethical commitments, presupposes that there is such a thing as *one's self* independent of one's social roles, and the transition from the ancient Greek understanding to our modern understanding is sometimes described as a move from 'pure role without self to pure self without role' (Hollis, 1996, pp. 91–108).

To see how important this move is, consider not only the extent to which Sophocles' Antigone exists as a function of her social position, but also the extent to which characters in Shakespeare's plays exist through their social roles – their gender, their race, their social status, and so on: Shylock is largely defined by his Jewishness, Lear by his status as King, Hamlet by his position as Prince of Denmark. In all these cases, social role is of very great importance, and what each must do is, in large part, a function of his or her social role. The tragedy of Romeo and Juliet arises almost entirely from the fact that the two lovers belong to warring families. However much they may wish to be individuals, they cannot escape their status as Montague and Capulet, respectively. Indeed, it is the naïve conviction that they can escape these roles which precipitates their death. Here is an extract from the famous balcony scene (Act 2, Scene 2):

Juliet: O Romeo, Romeo, wherefore art thou Romeo?
Deny thy father and refuse thy name;
Or if thou wilt not, be but sworn my love,
And I'll no longer be a Capulet.

Romeo: [*Aside*] Shall I hear more, or shall I speak at this?

Juliet: 'Tis but thy name that is my enemy:
Thou art thyself, though not a Montague.
What's Montague? It is nor hand nor foot
Nor arm nor face nor any other part
Belonging to a man. O be some other name.
What's in a name? That which we call a rose
By any other word would smell as sweet;
So Romeo would, were he not Romeo call'd,
Retain that dear perfection which he owes
Without that title. Romeo, doff thy name,
And for thy name, which is no part of thee,
Take all myself.

Romeo: I take thee at thy word:
Call me but love, and I'll be new baptis'd
Henceforth I never will be Romeo.

It is impossible for either Romeo or Juliet to 'doff' their names, and that fact is central to the play. What is possible for them, both individually and as a pair of lovers, is largely determined by the social circumstances in which they find themselves, and those circumstances include the fact that they are members of rival families. Even if they are not entirely defined by their social roles, Romeo and Juliet are severely circumscribed by them, and therein lies their tragedy.

However, as we move towards the modern period, social role seems to matter less and the self seems to matter more. The aspiration to shake off social role and transcend social position is prominent in modern literature, and indeed the novel is often understood as the literary manifestation of the growth of the individual. This is something which can be seen very clearly in, for example, the novels of Jane Austen, for one of the things that is noteworthy about Austen's heroines is that they strive to move beyond the confines of their social roles and to assert their own desires and values *as individuals*. In *Pride and Prejudice* Elizabeth Bennet refuses to accept her pre-assigned role as a wife, and insists on leading her own life and following her own values. Similarly the heroines of Henry James's novels are often characterized by their insistence on turning away from the expectations generated by social role. In *Portrait of a Lady*, Isabel Archer is determined to 'affront her destiny', by which she means that she will not be constrained by others' expectations of what is appropriate for a young woman in her position. And in philosophy, too, the movement towards the modern age is a movement in which the moral significance of social role or official position diminishes and is replaced by a growing sense of the importance of being a unique self – an individual.

Nonetheless, and whatever the 'direction of travel' in modern literature and philosophy, it is not clear that the notion of pure self without role is coherent, and Hollis goes so far as to suggest that reliance on it renders some moral philosophy (for example, utilitarianism) incoherent, too. The reason for this, Hollis says, is because it is not possible to answer questions about what one ought to do independent of a recognition of the social roles one occupies. The ambition of the moderns, as shown in both literature and philosophy, is to live a life unconstrained by social role or social expectation. It is to live a life that is authentically one's own and, as such, unconstrained by the demands of others, but such a life is, at the limit, unintelligible, and the reason for this is that, without a sense of the social roles we occupy, we have no way of answering questions about what we should do. The thought here is very like the thought expressed by Alasdair MacIntyre when he writes: 'I can only answer the question "what am I to do?" if I can answer the prior question "of what story or stories do I find myself a part?"' (MacIntyre, 1996, p. 216). In the absence of any understanding of myself as someone's mother, or someone's daughter, or someone's teacher, or someone's wife, I can have no sense of my 'self' nor therefore any sense of what I ought to do.

The point is perhaps best expressed via an example. It is tempting to think that in cases of conflict the best thing to do is the thing that will produce most happiness and least misery. So, although I do indeed occupy social roles, when those social roles conflict one with another, I ought to stand above them and decide, from a neutral vantage point, which action (of those available to me) will promote most happiness and least misery. However, this way of understanding the matter is not always helpful. Suppose that, as a young woman, I fervently desire academic success, but I also see that marriage to this man, whom I love very much, is likely to make academic success much less likely. I realize that if I marry, I will soon become content with domestic life and will abandon the ambitions which are now so important to me. Indeed, I will look back with pity on the ambitious young woman I once was and will be grateful that I am no longer in thrall to worldly goods but am fulfilled in my personal and domestic life. Should I marry?

The question cannot be answered by reference to what will make me happiest in the future, and the reason for this is that, in the example given, what will make me happiest in the future depends in part on what I decide now. To decide to marry is to take steps to ensure that my future happiness will be partly determined by domestic considerations, whereas to refrain from marrying is, in some part, to take steps to ensure that my future happiness will be partly determined by professional success. There is no antecedent and independent answer to the question 'What will make me happier?' for the question of what will make me happier in the future depends on the kind of person I will be in the future, and the kind of person I will be in the future depends (in part) on how I now decide. The general point that follows from this is that appeal to a self abstracted from all social considerations is not helpful in resolving this sort of dilemma, since this sort of dilemma raises, rather than answers, questions about the kind of person one is or is to become. It raises, and cannot presuppose, an understanding of the nature of the self.

What, though, are the implications of this for the central question of this book: 'How should we understand politicians' involvement in morally disreputable acts?' One implication is this: if we abandon the idea that we are selves independent of, or somehow 'beneath', the various roles we occupy, then it will not be possible to resolve conflicts of duty by appeal to individual conscience, or the dictates of the true self, or indeed by appeal to anything that goes beyond the duties that are attendant on office, social position, or social role, and this will be because, as the previous example suggested, the concept of the self is underdetermined. The question which stalks, therefore, is: 'How, in a world of plural and conflicting values, can we resolve the dilemmas that arise when values conflict with one another and, in particular, when the demands of office (including political office) conflict with what we, as individuals, believe to be morally right?'

In what follows I will address this question via a literary example. The example is given in Herman Melville's short novel *Billy Budd*, and I use it here because I believe it can illuminate the dilemmas faced when political office and private conscience conflict with one another and, in particular, can help us understand the position of the politician who finds that political duty requires him to do what he believes to be morally wrong.[1]

My discussion proceeds in the following stages: first, I give a brief account of the story told by Melville in *Billy Budd*; then I focus on the question of political morality as it is exemplified in the novel – that is to say, I focus on the question: 'What should the politician do when faced with a conflict between official duty and private conviction?' I then discuss several answers to this question before concluding with some general reflections on the way in which we might understand the involvement of politicians in morally disreputable acts. My aim throughout is to offer an answer to the question that has been central to this book: 'How should we understand the politician who does what is morally wrong?' First, though, the story of *Billy Budd*.

Billy Budd, sailor

Melville's novel is set in the year 1797. Britain is engaged
in a long and bitter war against France, and the British
war effort has been threatened by two naval mutinies – the
Nore Mutiny and the mutiny at Spithead. The action of
the novel takes place aboard His Majesty's Ship the *Indomitable*, and the central character of the novel is Billy Budd,
sailor. Billy Budd is a young man of exceptional beauty,
both physical and moral, whose only flaw is a stammer.
He is loved by all his fellow sailors except the master-
at-arms, John Claggart. The incarnation of evil, Claggart
recognizes in Billy the incarnation of goodness, and is
consumed by a jealousy which leads him to accuse Billy
(falsely) of inciting the crew to mutiny. Alone with Claggart and the ship's Captain, Edward Vere, Billy hears the
lying charge against him. He is enraged, but his stammer
prevents him from responding in words. He strikes Claggart, and the blow is fatal. Billy Budd, sailor, has killed
the master-at-arms of one of His Majesty's ships on active
service, and the penalty for this is death.

It now falls to Captain Vere to judge Billy Budd's case.
He knows Billy to be innocent of incitement to mutiny,
but he also knows that Billy has committed a capital
offence. How is he to proceed? Melville writes:

> In the jugglery of circumstances preceding and attending
> the event on board the *Indomitable*, and in the light of that
> martial code whereby it was formally to be judged, inno-
> cence and guilt...effectively changed places. In the legal
> view, the apparent victim of the tragedy was he [Claggart]
> who had sought to victimize a man blameless [Budd]; and
> the indisputable deed of the latter, navally regarded, con-
> stituted the most heinous of military crimes. (Melville,
> 1995, pp. 61–2)

Billy Budd is indeed 'innocent before God', but before man he is guilty. At the Last Assizes he will assuredly be acquitted, but it is God alone who can acquit. Man must condemn, and, reluctantly, Captain Vere condemns. He sentences Billy Budd to be hung at the yard-arm in the early morning watch. Billy's dying words are 'God bless Captain Vere'.

Billy Budd is in essence a novel about politics and about the responsibilities of political office. Captain Vere is a naval officer in time of war, he 'wears the King's buttons' and owes a duty to the King, but the King's edict here dictates that he hang a man whom he knows to be morally innocent. It dictates that he do something morally wrong. How are we to judge him and how is he to judge himself? These, of course, are the questions that have informed this book throughout. They are questions about the relationship between politics and morality; more precisely, they are questions about the extent to which we can reasonably expect that those who have political duties will be able to retain moral integrity.

In the remainder of this chapter I will suggest some ways in which we might understand and respond to the conflict between private conscience and political duty. To anticipate, there are those who believe that when faced with a choice between official duty and personal morality, the politician (Captain Vere) should choose official duty. On the other hand, there are those who believe that he (and we) should follow private conscience. Neither of these answers seems to me to be adequate: the former makes Vere a good officer, but a poor man, while the latter makes him a good man, but a poor officer. The challenge for Vere, however, is to be both a good man and a good officer. I will conclude, therefore, with a third answer, one which (I believe) enables us to see how it might be possible to be both, and how, therefore, we might understand the involvement of politicians in morally disreputable acts. I begin with the suggestion, foreshadowed by Machiavelli and prominent in other writers, too, that political actors ought to give priority to the demands made by their office.

Duties of office

The view that political actors ought to give priority to the duties of their office is not one that currently commands much support: it conjures up an image of the political actor as a mere functionary, hiding behind the demands of his official role with the largely disingenuous claim 'I was only obeying orders.' The list of those who have used this excuse is long and unedifying, and those of us old enough to remember the My Lai massacre are not, on the whole, sympathetic to it.

But our reaction is, in part, unfair and culturally specific. The Victorian writer James Fitzjames Stephen was clear that the duties of office take absolute priority over private conscience, and he offers reasons for that view which are interesting and instructive. Discussing the case of Pontius Pilate (the case on which some say *Billy Budd* is based), Stephen writes: 'The point to which I wish to direct attention is that Pilate's duty was to maintain peace and order in Judea and to uphold the Roman power....to a man in Pilate's position the morals and the social order which he represents are for all practical purposes final and absolute standards' (Stephen, 1967, p. 114). And he continues:

> If this should appear harsh, I would appeal to Indian experience. Suppose that some great religious reformer – say, for instance, someone claiming to be the Guru of the Sikhs, or the Imam in whose advent many Mahommedans

believe – were to make his appearance in the Punjab. Suppose that there was good reason to believe that whatever might be the preacher's personal intentions, his preaching was calculated to disturb the public peace and produce mutiny and rebellion: and suppose further that a British officer, instead of doing whatever might be necessary, or executing whatever orders he might receive, for the maintenance of British authority, were to consider whether or not he ought to become a disciple of the Guru or Imam. What course would be taken towards him? He would be instantly dismissed with ignominy from the service which he would disgrace, and if he acted up to his convictions, and preferred his religion to his Queen and country, he would be hanged as a rebel and a traitor. (Stephen, 1967, pp. 115–16)

'And quite right, too', Stephen implies.

It is tempting to dismiss these remarks as simply an expression of Victorian jingoism – exactly the views one would expect from a nineteenth-century defender of Queen and Empire. And in part, that's what they are. They do, however, have an interest beyond the merely parochial. Stephen's conclusion that politics is of su)reme importance is based on a general moral claim that 'to a man in Pilate's position the morals and the social order which he represents are for all practical purposes final and absolute standards'. To hold an official position (a political position), whether as Roman Governor of Judea, or as Captain of HMS *Indomitable,* is not simply to have official (in these cases, political) duties, it is also to represent, in one's own person, the moral standards of the society to which one belongs. On this understanding, Pontius Pilate, as Governor of Judea, is the personification of Roman morality, and Roman views about justice. Similarly, Captain Vere is the personification of the moral values that prompted and informed the war against France. This may seem hideously over-stated: surely, it cannot be the case that in taking on an official responsibility one becomes nothing other than the mouthpiece of the establishment? We are inclined to think that it cannot, but I believe that we are in part deceived and that Stephen articulates an important truth.

That truth is that when we accept official roles, we thereby become, to some considerable extent, the representative of and spokesperson for the body that appoints us. As Roman Governor of Judea, Pontius Pilate speaks for Rome in Judea; as Captain of HMS *Indomitable,* Captain Vere speaks for the King. To move from the sublime to the ridiculous, as Head of Department, I speak for my department. And crucially, I do that (or should do that) independent of whether the views of the department are my personal views. For sure, I need not think – and do not think – that I am the mere puppet of those in whose name I act, but equally, having taken on an official role, I cannot simply distance myself from the views of those whom I represent. And 'cannot' here means 'morally cannot'.

To see how this is so, consider the moral status of resignation. It is sometimes (often) said that, if a person's official or political role requires him to do things he believes to be morally wrong, then it is always open to him to resign and, thus, the implication is, to escape responsibility for what subsequently happens. This strikes me as both false and naïve. There can of course be cases in which resignation exculpates, but more often responsibility survives resignation, albeit the responsibility is of a rather different kind.

In his discussion of the problem of dirty hands, Martin Hollis refers to those German judges who were appointed under the Weimar Republic and subsequently found themselves called upon to administer anti-Semitic laws. He notes that:

Some resigned but others, reckoning that they would merely be replaced by ardent Nazis, stayed on, grimly trying to do some slight good. Whether or not they made the right choice, they were certainly right about the responsibility. Those who resigned escaped the office, but not the responsibility.... Once a dilemma has been posed for a person in office, integrity does not demand that he keep his hands clean by stepping aside. It is too late for clean hands, whatever he does. (Hollis, 1996, p. 143)

There are, it seems to me, two ways in which this is true, two ways in which responsibility survives resignation. First, when we accept official positions we know that they carry responsibilities with them and, unless we are very naïve, we know that those responsibilities will sometimes require us to do what we believe to be morally wrong. To agree to take on an official role just is to accept that one will be bound by its duties even when they are morally disagreeable. Of course, there are limits to this, and when those limits are exceeded, people may feel that the only honourable course is resignation. However, and this is the second point, even when the limits are exceeded, responsibility does not evaporate entirely, for one continues to bear some responsibility for what happens as a result of one's own refusal to carry on. This is not, it must be emphasized, a defence of utilitarianism. I am not suggesting that, in general, when I refuse to do something I believe to be wrong, I am thereby responsible for the terrible things that other people do in response. What I am suggesting is that official duties make a difference and that, when I resign rather than do what my official duty dictates, I cannot 'wash my hands' of the consequences that follow from that resignation, for resignation is, by definition, a way of rejecting the moral duties I took upon myself when I accepted office. It may be that the rejection is justified; it may be that it is the honourable thing to do. But the person who resigns, and thus abdicates responsibility, is not in the same moral position as the person who never had that responsibility in the first place.

In short, then, the view that the political actor has a responsibility to do what the duties of his office dictate, and that he has that responsibility even when the duties conflict with his own conscience, is not without merit. Nonetheless, it is not, to my mind, fully satisfactory, for the initial objection – that this threatens to make the officer a mere functionary or puppet – persists.

This brings me to the second of the two views mentioned at the outset – the view that, when political duty and private conscience conflict, one should follow private conscience. So, in this case – the case of *Billy Budd* – Captain Vere should refuse to sentence Billy Budd to death.

Demands of conscience

One writer who emphasizes the importance of individual conscience in cases of conflict is David Wiggins, when he writes:

> Even if Vere would have put his commission at risk in not proceeding so summarily against Billy Budd (because there was some just appreciable risk of indiscipline or disorder ensuing, for which he would have been held responsible), well – in the name of natural justice, never mind Vere's mental dispositions or the orderly unfolding of his life-plan (doomed in any case, to judge from the story) – perhaps that risk ought to have been taken. And the thought that it ought to have been taken was open to Vere. (Wiggins, 1987, p. 180)

By contrast with Stephen, Wiggins insists that it is appropriate, indeed morally obligatory, to take a 'provisional' attitude towards the duties of one's official role. The duties of one's official role are, of course, moral duties, but we must always reserve the right to renounce them if they conflict with our understanding of natural justice. So, Pontius Pilate should not see himself simply as Roman Governor of Judea, nor should Vere see himself simply as captain of HMS *Indomitable*. Each should remain himself and should be ready to bring the moral demands of office before a higher court – the court of his own moral judgement. Generalizing the point, it seems that, for Wiggins, politicians who find that the duties of office require them to do what is morally wrong should stand back from those duties and contemplate renouncing them and doing what their own moral code dictates.

Again, this understanding of the relationship between self and official role has some intuitive plausibility: as noted earlier, when we appoint people to public office we want them to be more than mere conduits for the demands made by that office, and there is something alarming about a person who is never prepared to put into question the obligations that fall upon him in his official capacity. More than that, there is reason for not entrusting such a person with public office in the first place.

However, Wiggins' appeal to conscience is not without difficulty. I have already noted some reservations about the coherence of a move from 'pure role without self to pure self without role', but there are at least two further problems with the suggestion that, in cases of conflict, we should prioritize individual conscience. The first problem is that individual conscience is notoriously unreliable, and indeed duties of office are themselves a way of trying to limit the scope for its exercise. This may be because political agents have to act, as did Vere, in the 'obscuring smoke' of battle: we all know that our own judgement is unreliable when we are 'under fire', whether the fire is physical or metaphorical, and, for that reason, the moment when we are tempted to ignore the duties of office is likely to be the moment when we should pay most attention to them.

Beyond that, however, we have good reason for refusing to appoint to office a man who declares that, when the duties of office conflict with his conscience, he will follow his conscience. This is not simply because such a statement suggests that he does not take his office and its duties morally seriously, it is also because we have no assurance that conscience tells him (or us) the right thing.

There is a classic statement of this problem in Mark Twain's *Huckleberry Finn*. Set in nineteenth-century Missouri, the novel tells how a young white boy (Huck Finn) helps Jim, the black slave, to escape from his owner, Miss Watson. As the raft sails down the Mississippi, bringing Jim closer and closer to freedom, Huck realizes what he has done. He has stolen someone else's property. Here are his thoughts:

> Jim said it made him all over trembly and feverish to be so close to freedom. Well, I can tell you it made me all over trembly and feverish, too, to hear him, because I begun to get it through my head that he was most free – and who was to blame for it? Why, *me*. I couldn't get that out of my conscience no how nor no way...it hadn't ever come home to me before what this thing was that I was doing. But now it did; and it stayed with me and scorched me more and more. (Twain, 1966, Chapter 16)

Conscience speaks clearly to Huck and tells him that he has done wrong. Things get worse when Jim announces his intention to buy his wife and children out of slavery; and then adds that, if the children cannot be bought, he will steal them. Huck is horrified:

> Thinks I, this is what comes of my not thinking. Here was this nigger which I had as good as helped to run away, coming right out flat-footed and saying he would steal his children – children that belonged to a man I didn't even know; a man that hadn't ever done me no harm.
> I was sorry to hear Jim say that, it was such a lowering of him. My conscience got to me and stirred me up hotter than ever, until at last I says to it, 'Let up on me – it ain't too late, yet – I'll paddle ashore at first light and tell'. I felt easy, and happy and light as a feather, right off. All my troubles was gone. (Twain, 1966, Chapter 16)

We, I take it, think that Huck should dismiss the dictates of conscience, for conscience can be a bad guide as well as a good one, and we do well to remember that before we rush to applaud the person who follows conscience, much less to insist that, when conscience and official duty conflict, we ought to give priority to conscience. The case is more complex than that simple response implies.

Throughout this book my concern has been with the question of whether politicians can be morally good and, in particular, with the question of how they (and we) might understand cases in which the demands of political office conflict with what is, or at least seems to be, morally right. In the preceding discussion, I indicated that neither an insistence on the primacy of office, nor an insistence on the priority of conscience is ultimately satisfactory. How, then, should we understand the conflict? In the next section I offer a tentative suggestion.

Duty and diversity

In his 1987 essay 'The Idea of an Overlapping Consensus', John Rawls tells us that 'the aims of political philosophy depend on the society it addresses' (Rawls, 1999, p. 421), and he then goes on to note that modern liberal societies are characterized by the fact and permanence of pluralism. In speaking of pluralism, Rawls is not using the term in the same way as Berlin. That is to say, he is not claiming that there are plural sets of values and that those sets of values conflict with one another in an ultimate and irresoluble way such that 'one must choose between them and having chosen not look back'. Rawls' claim is a much more modest one and is based on the simple recognition that modern societies (particularly Western liberal societies) contain people of many different races, different religions, different cultural commitments, different moral and political beliefs. In short, modern societies contain people of many different ways of life and, although it *may* be true that these different ways of life ultimately conflict with one another, Rawls himself has nothing to say about that possibility, but simply contents himself with the reflection that we live in plural societies and that we have no reason to think that that pluralism will disappear.

Now, in insisting on the fact and permanence of pluralism, Rawls is thinking primarily of the different *groups* of people which go to make up a society such as Britain or the United States in the twenty-first century: Muslims differ from Christians; the Amish differ from secular liberals; hedonists differ from environmentalists, and so on. What is also true, however, is that individuals differ one from another, and may legitimately come to different conclusions about the best way to lead one's life. Consider John Stuart Mill's famous claim:

If a person possesses any tolerable amount of common sense and experience, his own mode of laying out his existence is best, not because it is the best in itself, but because it is his own mode. Human beings are not like sheep, and even sheep are not indistinguishably alike. A man cannot get a coat or a pair of boots to fit him unless they are either made to his measure or he has a whole warehouseful to choose from; and is it easier to fit him with a life than with a coat? (Mill, 1978b, pp. 132–3)

What Mill implies is that what is right for one man may be wrong for another, and Rawls concurs with this when he notes that one reason why we cannot expect convergence on moral judgement is because 'different conceptions of the world can reasonably be elaborated from different standpoints and diversity arises in part from our different perspectives. It is unrealistic – or worse, it arouses mutual suspicion and hostility – to suppose that all our differences are rooted solely in ignorance and perversity, or else in the rivalries for power, status, or economic gain' (Rawls, 1993, p. 58).

So Mill and Rawls are as one in thinking that differences of opinion about what is right (what is the right way to lead one's life, what is the right way to worship, what is the highest ideal in life) are to be expected. For Rawls such differences are the predictable outcome of the operation of reason under conditions of freedom, and for Mill they are a sign of a society which shows proper respect for diversity and individuality. More generally, it is not only Rawls and Mill who insist on, and indeed applaud, societal diversity; it is also liberals quite generally, since liberalism as a political theory begins precisely from the recognition that people are different from one another and are therefore unlikely to converge on answers to difficult moral problems.

What, though, does this have to do with our central question: how – in general – should we understand the involvement of politicians in morally disreputable acts, and how – in particular – should we understand Captain Vere's decision to order the death of Billy Budd? So far, the discussion of this question has covered two possibilities: the first is that, in cases of conflict, official duty should take priority over private conscience; the second is that, in cases of conflict, private conscience should take priority over official duty. For reasons already given, neither alternative is fully satisfactory, and the introduction of liberal pluralism draws our attention to the possibility that, in the final analysis, there may be no single right answer, and that the question of what it is right for Captain Vere to do will depend, in part, on his character and personality, for it is a basic premise of modern liberalism, with its commitment to the permanence of pluralism, that something may be right for one person, given his dispositions, character, cultural background, moral commitments, and so on, but not right for someone whose dispositions, character, cultural background, and moral commitments are different. So, a satisfactory answer to the question 'What ought Captain Vere to do?' may require essential reference to his character and personality, and also to the historical and cultural circumstances in which his decision is taken. And generalizing from this, we may find that a satisfactory answer to questions about the proper balance between official duty and private conscience may not admit of a single answer, but may be dependent on context and personality.

The reason for this, I suggest, is that when people are appointed to public office, they are appointed within a context that defines – to a greater or lesser extent – not only what the duties of office are, but also, and crucially, how they themselves should relate to those duties. When

I take on an official role, I accept specific duties, but I also accept, or offer, an understanding of my relationship to those duties, and that understanding will differ from one historical moment to another, from one cultural context to another, and from one individual to another. For a man in Pontius Pilate's position, the duties of office were indeed absolute. In becoming Roman Governor of Judea, he undertook to speak with the voice of Rome. For us, things are rather different: we have different duties and, crucially, different understandings of our relationship to those duties. These are the differences of standpoint or perspective which underpin the permanence of pluralism. However, they are not differences that amount simply to differences of conscience. They are differences that inform our understanding of the moral status of the exercise of conscience.

To put the point differently, when we appoint people to political office we do so against a background understanding of both their own personality (their perspective or standpoint or conception of the good) and the stringency of the requirements of the post. Sometimes, we appoint those who are more likely to exercise their own judgement; sometimes we don't. Sometimes we ourselves are appointed because we are independent spirits; sometimes we are passed over for that very same reason. Having once been appointed because we have a particular standpoint or perspective, it is not open to us to deliberate, as if *de novo*, on our relationship to the duties of office. That was, in part, something we committed to at the outset.

The dilemma of Captain Vere arises most acutely when he is appointed because he is, or is deemed to be, a man of judgement, and not a mere 'rule follower', for now he has specific duties arising from his role as captain of the

Indomitable (the duty to comply with the requirements of the Mutiny Act, for instance), but he also, and legitimately, has an understanding of himself as someone who has been made captain *precisely because* he will not always obey those duties. He has been appointed not as mere rule follower but as a man of judgement – one who recognizes that rules are for the guidance of wise men. For such a man, the question is not 'What is it right for the Captain of HMS *Indomitable* to do?' (the question is not a simple question about official duty), nor is it 'what is it right for me to do?' (it is not a simple question about private conscience). Rather, the question is 'What is it right for me as Captain of HMS *Indomitable* to do?', where that question emphasizes both that Vere has official duties and that he has been appointed because we know that he will perceive those duties from his distinctive perspective or standpoint. And if he were not inclined to do that, we would not have appointed him in the first place.

There is, then, no general answer to questions about the way in which private conscience ought to be weighed against official role, and the reason for this is not simply that the demands of a role differ from time to time and from place to place, but also (and crucially) because there are many cases in which the duties are not fully specified in advance but must themselves be arrived at by the judicious reasoning of the office holder, and in a world where different office holders will legitimately and predictably reason differently.

It may be thought that this is not an answer to our central question, but a refusal to answer it. Perhaps. But if we take seriously the fact that different people will have different moral ideals, and if we recognize that that fact is the central fact for Western liberal democracies, then we will wish to allow room for differences of judgement amongst politicians just as much as amongst other members of society.

Conclusion

The central question of this book has been: 'Are politicians morally worse than the rest of us?' I began by noting the claim that it is more difficult for politicians to stand by their own moral and ethical commitments since politics requires heightened attention to consequences and heightened impartiality. The demands of impartiality and of attention to consequences, when taken together, make it very difficult for politicians to retain their integrity, or so it is claimed. In order to assess the claim, I have discussed three ways in which integrity may be undermined: the first is by the demands of consequentialism, the second is through value pluralism, and the third is via the conflicts that arise when private conscience and social role conflict one with another. However, in each case I have suggested that, in the final analysis, the politician may be very similar to all the rest of us. Insofar as we all occupy official positions, we may all find that we cannot always act according to the dictates of our private conscience but must also acknowledge the duties attached to our social role; insofar as we recognize the existence of different and conflicting values, we may all find that we must, from time to time, sacrifice something of ethical value; insofar as we have concern for things outside ourselves, we may all find that consequences must occasionally be given priority over our own commitments and ideals. In these ways, we all live, as Taylor puts it 'between the one and the many', though of course the stakes may be very much higher for the politician, the temptations greater, and the costs of error more public. Enoch Powell once, and famously, declared 'all

Chapter 3   Integrity and Utilitarianism

1   It may be objected that I am vacillating here between politicians and public officials. This is true, but not, I think, damaging. Both the politician and the public official act on behalf of us (the citizens) and, in that sense, they are *our* agents (see Hollis, 1996, p. 137).

Chapter 4   Integrity and Pluralism

1   Broadly speaking, value pluralism holds that the sources of value are many and not one. It is to be contrasted with the 'fact of pluralism' as that term is used in John Rawls' later writings, especially *Political Liberalism* (1993). For the classic statement of Berlin's value pluralism, see his 'Two Concepts of Liberty' in *Four Essays on Liberty* (1969). For an admirably clear statement of the differences between the fact of pluralism and value pluralism see Charles Larmore, *The Morals of Modernity* (1996), Chapter 7, 'Pluralism and Reasonable Disagreement'.

2   At http://209.85.229.132/search?q=cache:pq_9LTzIrLAJ: www.wsu.edu/~dee/GREECE/PERICLES.HTM+ thucydides+such+was+the+end+of+these+men&cd=1&hl= en&ct=clnk&gl=uk (accessed 21 May 2009).

3   Of course, if the politician fails to abide by the values of politics, then he will lose integrity. If, for instance, he refuses to authorize torture even though that is what politics requires, he will lose integrity as a politician but he may, perhaps, gain integrity of another sort. It may therefore be that, even on a pluralist account, integrity is at risk for the politician. I am grateful to Cecle Fabre for drawing this possibility to my attention.

Chapter 5   Integrity and Social Roles

1   The discussion here draws on my article 'Innocent Before God: Politics, Morality and the Case of Billy Budd' (2006).

References

Alterman, Eric (2005) *When Presidents Lie: A History of Official Deception and Its Consequences*, Harmondsworth: Penguin

Anscombe, G.E.M. (1981) 'Mr Truman's Degree', in G.E.M. Anscombe, *Ethics, Religion and Politics: Collected Philosophical Papers, Vol. III*, Oxford: Blackwell

Bennett, Jonathan (1974) 'The Conscience of Huckleberry Finn', *Philosophy*, Vol. 49, pp. 123–34

Berlin, Isaiah (1969) *Four Essays on Liberty*, Oxford: Oxford University Press

Berlin, Isaiah (1992) 'The Question of Machiavelli', in Robert Adams (ed.), *The Prince*, New York and London: Norton

Calhoun, Cheshire (1995) 'Standing for Something', *Journal of Philosophy*, Vol. XCII, No. 5, May, pp. 235–60

Carritt, E.F. (1963) *Ethical and Political Thinking*, Oxford: Clarendon

Flynt, Larry (2005) *Sex, Lies and Politics: The Naked Truth about Bush, Democracy and the War on Terror*, London, Kensington Books

Goodin, Robert (1995) 'Government House Utilitarianism', in Robert Goodin, *Utilitarianism as a Public Philosophy*, Cambridge: Cambridge University Press

Hampshire, Stuart (1992) *Innocence and Experience*, Harmondsworth: Penguin

Hollis, Martin (1996) *Reason in Action: Essays in the Philosophy of Social Science*, Cambridge: Cambridge University Press

Larmore, Charles (1996) *The Morals of Modernity*, Cambridge: Cambridge University Press

McFall, Lynne (1987) 'Integrity', *Ethics*, Vol. 98, pp. 5–27

Machiavelli, Niccolò (1961) *The Prince*, edited and translated by George Bull, Harmondsworth: Penguin

MacIntyre, Alasdair (1996) *After Virtue: A Study in Moral Theory*, London: Duckworth

Melville, Herman (1995) *Billy Budd, Sailor*, Harmondsworth: Penguin

Mendus, Susan (2006) 'Innocent before God: Politics, Morality and the Case of Billy Budd', in Anthony O'Hear (ed.), *Political Philosophy*, Cambridge: Cambridge University Press

Mendus, Susan (2008) 'Life's Ethical Symphony', *Journal of Philosophy of Education*, Vol. 42, No. 2, pp. 201–18

Mill, John Stuart (1978a) *Utilitarianism*, edited by Mary Warnock, London: Fontana

Mill, John Stuart (1978b) *On Liberty*, edited by Gertrude Himmelfarb, Harmondsworth: Penguin

Nagel, Thomas (1978) 'Ruthlessness in Public Life', in Stuart Hampshire (ed.), *Public and Private Morality*, Cambridge: Cambridge University Press

Newbold, Stephanie (2005) 'Statesmanship and Ethics: The Case of Thomas Jefferson's Dirty Hands', *Public Administration Review*, Vol. 65, No. 6, November/December, pp. 669–75.

Oborne, Peter (2005) *The Rise of Political Lying*, London: Free Press

Plato (1974) *Republic*, translated by E.V. Rieu, Harmondsworth: Penguin

Rawls, John (1971) *A Theory of Justice*, Cambridge, MA: Harvard, University Press

Rawls, John (1993) *Political Liberalism*, Cambridge, MA: Harvard University Press

Rawls, John (1999) 'The Idea of an Overlapping Consensus', in Samuel Freeman (ed.), *John Rawls: Collected Papers*, Cambridge, MA: Harvard University Press

Richards, Norvin (1992) *Humility*, Philadelphia: Temple University Press

Saxonhouse, Arlene W. (2004) 'Corruption and Justice: The View from Ancient Athens', in William C. Heffernann and John Kleinig (eds), *Private and Public Corruption*, London, Rowman and Littlefield

Shirer, William L. (1991) *Rise and Fall of the Third Reich*, London: Arrow

Stephen, James Fitzjames (1967) *Liberty, Equality, Fraternity*, Cambridge: Cambridge University Press

Styron, William (1979) *Sophie's Choice*, London: Jonathan Cape

Taylor, Charles (1997) 'Leading a Life', in Ruth Chang (ed.), *Incommensurability, Incomparability, and Practical Reason*, Cambridge, MA: Harvard University Press

Thompson, Dennis (1987) *Political Ethics and Public Office*, Cambridge, MA: Harvard University Press

Twain, Mark (1966) *Huckleberry Finn*, Harmondsworth: Penguin

Walzer, Michael (1974) 'Political Action: The Problem of Dirty Hands', in Marshall Cohen, Thomas Nagel and Thomas Scanlon (eds), *War and Moral Responsibility*, Princeton, NJ: Princeton University Press

Wiggins, David (1987) 'Truth, and Truth as Predicated of Moral Judgements', in David Wiggins, *Need, Values, Truth*, Oxford, Blackwell

Williams, Bernard (1973) 'A Critique of Utilitarianism', in Bernard Williams and J.J.C. Smart, *Utilitarianism: For and Against*, Cambridge: Cambridge University Press

Williams, Bernard (1981) *Moral Luck*, Cambridge: Cambridge University Press

Williams, Bernard (1995) 'Replies', in J.E.J. Altham and Ross Harrison (eds), *World, Mind, and Ethics: Essays on the Ethical Philosophy of Bernard Williams*, Cambridge: Cambridge University Press

Index